YOUTH FACE TODAY'S ISSUES 1

Adapted for youth from the best-selling
FACING THE ISSUES Series

WILLIAM J. KRUTZA
AND PHILIP P. DI CICCO

Contemporary
Discussion Series

Baker Book House
Grand Rapids, Michigan 49506

Your World – Welcome to It!

FACING THE ISSUES – that's exactly what many youth say adults aren't doing. For some dissidents, everything is wrong with the world, and it's all the fault of those over thirty. Suddenly the world has gone all in the wrong direction. It either has to be changed or destroyed. Unfortunately, the destroyers seem to be getting more publicity than the changers. Of course, it's easier to bomb a building than change the attitudes of the people who work inside. It's easier to destroy a university than help it become a strong force for constructive change in society. Destruction is immediate; change takes time. Unfortunately, too many youth don't like to wait.

Christian youth are caught between the stability of their church life and the changeability of the issues of society. Because the church doesn't dive into every issue, some feel the church isn't saying enough about what's going on. If you're of that breed, remember that you are a part of the church. You are criticizing yourself as well as others. Is that what you really want to say – "I'm at fault?" If not, what are your constructive, life-changing, absolutely certain answers to all the issues of our society? And why haven't you given these answers to the world? Really, how many issues do you talk about with sufficient meaning to bring about an-

1

swers? Make a list of all the issues you really haven't solved. Quite a list, isn't it?

That's what this book is all about — facing issues from a youthful point of view. The twelve issues in this book aren't all the issues in the world, by far. But it's a good start. Most likely there are issues here that you've never discussed before. And if you have, you probably haven't come up with one really earth-shaking solution. Join the crowd — it's your world. Welcome to it!

Why discuss issues? Basically because issues demand answers. We give an answer even when we say nothing about a problem. Silence can be one answer. But it's not usually youth's answer. And we'd rather you take the coffee-house approach — everyone speak up. Our fast-paced world constantly presents new areas of living that demand the development and application of moral and scriptural guidelines. Almost every week something new crops up — and if you as an under-thirty person are going to answer the world's great problems, you'd better keep busy tackling some of the everyday variety.

Possibly you've given a lot of superficial answers to the weighty issues of our society. Youth have a tendency to give stock answers, especially when they can blame adults for the mess we are in. As you delve into this book you'll find that blaming anyone isn't the answer we need, nor will you be able to come up with one-sentence answers. You'll enter into an exciting approach to life — not only identifying problems, but brainstorming to find Christian answers.

Who doesn't have *problems!* It's *answers* we need. And since it takes so few years to make an adult out of you, you'll soon be in the position where others will be looking at you as either the cause or the cure of the world's ills. Enter the door of discussion with others in your group and you'll be on the road to providing some answers.

This book isn't designed to give you the answers to the issues. Its purpose is to state the case from a variety of viewpoints and then let you come up with the answer that best fits your situation. Pay particular attention to the "What Does the Bible Say?" sections. The Bible doesn't come out with dogmatic statements of conduct in every case, but it does provide those principles which can answer the knotty problems of today. If the Bible is absolutely clear on a subject, there's no issue about it. You will have to dig into the Scriptures even beyond the verses listed from the two modern versions to find fully satisfying answers. Don't neglect this important part of your preparation for the discussion. The Bible will provide those timeless principles that will help you establish the best approaches to your world.

It really is your world. The issues are yours to face. What will your answers be? By honest searching and open discussion of the issues in this book, it is hoped that you will be better prepared to live in your world. Then you'll be more eager to tell others, "Welcome to it!"

Contents

Poverty — Whose Problem? 1

MOST OF US WHO READ THIS BOOK are part of the affluent society. Either our parents or we have sufficient income to pay for our basic needs and some luxuries. Verbally we rebel against affluence, yet we take advantage of all it affords. America has given us the opportunity to earn enough money to satisfy our demands. Yet there are about twenty-two million Americans who subsist at a "poverty level."

In some sections of our great country, children are badly undernourished, subject to disease, without proper medical help, and some are near starvation. That just isn't fair. Yet, most young people who crowd their way into the nearest drive-in restaurant, like the adults before them, do little to change the situation. Possibly the main reason is that too few of us are interested in making any real sacrifice for the poor. Few of us care enough to learn of poverty on a person-to-person involvement basis.

United States government statistics reveal that one-tenth of Americans live at the poverty level. This level is based on family income of $3,000 or less a year. It's difficult to believe these statistics. Many teen-agers earn more than $3,000 and keep it for themselves apart from family income!

Michael Harrington, in his book, *The Other America,* says that the solution to the poverty problem is to have the government apportion out more money. He says that we have to do more than tell the poor that they are better off than the Indian poor, the Russian poor, or the Italian poor. He suggests that our standard of compassion should not be how much worse things could be, but how much better.

One of the world's greatest problems is that while some countries are experiencing fantastic modernization and advancement, others, because of exploding populations and poor education, are becoming increasingly poverty dominated. Americans who have undergone the revolution of modernization often do not understand why so much of the world seems so slow to catch up. One of our greatest problems is that we have become computerized. Some feel that the computer has replaced compassion — especially in dealing with those at the poverty level. The gap between the rich nations and the poor nations is one of the most tragic and urgent problems of the world.

Communists have advanced a rather simplistic answer — one that has appeal to those who are starving: take away from the "haves" and give to the "have nots." Many American youth are proposing this philosophy with little or no examination. They haven't studied the results of communism in the countries where it is the dominating governmental force. Rather than eliminating poverty in the countries in which it has gained control, communism has often caused the people to remain at a near subsistence level. Especially compared with the living standards practiced in America, the poverty levels of most people in communistic societies is obvious. To succumb to this simplistic propaganda will only aggravate the poverty problem, especially in a free society.

What is needed? What can Christians do to bring about a better balance between the rich and the poor? Should Christians become modern Robin Hoods to rob the rich and give to the poor? Is there a simplistic answer to the problem of poverty? If so, how will it work?

We have the resources available in America to eliminate poverty. We can see to it that people who can't change their circumstances can at least have adequate housing and food. We can sacrifice for their benefit. We can give of our lives to help train them so they can become productive citizens in the mainstream of American life.

What we need is the moral courage to do these things. But it'll take a reversing of our attitudes. Young people, who'll inherit the problems in a few years, must come up with adequate solutions. It will require more than campus rhetoric. It will require sacrifices and concern. It will require generosity and a tightening of the affluent belts of youth and adults. Are you willing to really help solve our poverty problem?

Generosity is the best policy. Each one giving of his affluence and influence. Each seeking opportunities to express self-giving love. Each one affording freedom for the poverty stricken to enter into the mainstream of life.

Poverty isn't a new invention. It's as old as mankind. Even Jesus stated, "The poor you always have with you." But the fact that former generations ignored the problem doesn't give the now generation the same right.

Unfortunately, many Bible-believing Christians have remained aloof toward poverty. They have been suspicious of any program to relieve the poor. They cite the first-century Christians who took care of those in need. The early church had its own seemingly efficient antipoverty program. Why shouldn't the church simply reestablish this approach? Why does the government have to give the answer to this gigantic problem when the church already possesses the answer?

Evangelicals have always championed the free enterprise system. They have opposed welfare programs because such programs tend to stymie individual initiative. Unfortunately, too many who have made it on their own still believe that anyone can make it. Although most suburban youth have known nothing but the affluent life (courtesy of their parents), they also maintain that anyone who works hard enough can become affluent in today's society.

Some believe that a person is poor more by choice than by circumstances. Many hold that the poor are poor because they are lazy. Some of this *is* true — but simply because poverty does not inspire ambition. Poverty does not generate initiative. So the answer to the problem is made more complex because society must help the poor not only to have a higher subsistence level but to challenge them to higher motivation levels.

Christians must realize that poverty is more than a political problem that can be solved with vast amounts of money. It will not be solved by the simplistic communistic ideas of reducing the rich to the level of the poor. Poverty contains moral and spiritual aspects. As Rufus Jones points out, "Poverty breaks the spirit and destroys the initiative of its victims." The Christian young person has to couple moral and spiritual renewal with political involvement. He has to help the "have nots" gain the self-respect needed to develop mentally, psychologically, and in relation to God to the point that they'll accept the challenges of greater purpose and industry. The Christian has also to supply the circumstances for equality that will allow such attitudes.

The question for Christian youth is: Where do we start? Do we start by demonstrating in front of the mayor's office? Should we start by marching to Washington? Do we start by asking the government to solve the problem with bigger and better programs? Should we start by burning down the welfare department buildings? Should we start by giving help on a volunteer basis to reach ghetto youth with better education? Should we start by sacrificing some of the luxuries of life and giving our time to help the underprivileged gain the means to obtain luxuries for themselves?

WHAT DOES THE BIBLE SAY?

"When there is among you a poor man . . . you shall not harden your heart or close your hand for your poor brother, refusing him a loan; no, you shall open wide your hand for him and lend him liberally to meet his need amply. Be on your guard . . . so that you [not] turn a loveless eye on your poor brother, and you give him nothing. He will cry out to the Lord against you, and it will become sin in you. You shall make the loan to him freely, not heavy of heart when you give to him . . . The land will never be without its poor, so I command you to be openhanded towards your brother, to the needy, and to the poor in the land" (Deut. 15:7-11).

"He who gives to the poor will not lack, and he who hides his eyes will receive many curses" (Prov. 28:27).

"Once a man came to Jesus. 'Teacher,' he asked, 'what good thing must I do to receive eternal life?' . . . Jesus said to him, 'If you want to be perfect, go and sell all you have and give the money to the poor, and you will have riches in heaven; then come and follow me'" (Matt. 19:16-21).

"Then the King will say to the people on his right: 'You who are blessed by my Father: come! Come and receive the kingdom which has been prepared for you ever since the creation of the world. I was hungry and you fed me, thirsty and you gave me drink;

I was a stranger and you received me in your homes, naked and you clothed me. . . I tell you, indeed, whenever you did this for one of the least important of these brothers of mine, you did it for me!' " (Matt. 25:34-40).

"All the believers continued together in close fellowship and shared their belongings with one another. They would sell their property and possessions and distribute the money among all, according to what each one needed" (Acts 2:44, 45).

"My brothers! In your life as believers in our Lord Jesus Christ, the Lord of glory, you must never treat people in different ways because of their outward appearance. Suppose a rich man wearing a gold ring and fine clothes comes in to your meeting, and a poor man in ragged clothes also comes in. If you show more respect to the well-dressed man and say to him, 'Have this best seat here,' but say to the poor man, 'Stand, or sit down here on the floor by my seat,' then you are guilty of creating distinctions among yourselves and making judgments based on evil motives. Listen, my dear brothers! God chose the poor people of this world to be rich in faith and to possess the Kingdom which he promised to those who love him. But you dishonor the poor! Who oppresses you and drags you before the judges? The rich! They are the ones who speak evil of that good name which God has given you. You will be doing the right thing if you obey the law of the Kingdom, which is found in the scripture, 'Love your neighbor as yourself'" (James 2:1-8).

WHAT DO YOU SAY?

1. What is poverty? How do you define it? Does it relate solely to money and things?

2. Jesus said, "You will always have poor people with you" (Mark 14:7). Does this mean we should simply recognize this as their lot in life? Why or why not?

3. Since welfare programs are the work of present governments, what should a local church or local youth group do about the poverty problem? What positive things can your group do besides talk about it?

4. Does the Bible support the idea of helping those in poverty? Give a few Bible illustrations. Was the sharing practiced in Acts 7 by the early Christians a form of social welfare? If so, should this be continued in a like form today? Why or why not?

5. Why do many conservative Christians oppose governmental welfare programs? Discuss the pros as well as the cons of their attitudes. Determine what your stance is.

6. Can we place some of the blame for poverty on the poor? Why or why not?

7. Jesus told the rich young ruler to sell his possessions and give to the poor. Could this seemingly simple approach be applied today? How? Can we follow Jesus fully without getting involved in helping the needy around us?

8. Can you truly be concerned about the souls of poor people without being concerned about their physical needs? Be sure to read I John 3:17, 18 here.

9. Should your local church or youth group originate an agency to take care of the poor in your community? How would this organization operate? Where would you get the money? When will you get started?

10. What are you personally doing to help some poor people in your community? What is your youth group doing? What could it do?

Should Christians Ever Disobey Laws? 2

DISSENT SEEMS TO BE ONE OF American youth's cherished pastimes. The right to protest and dissent is an American freedom exercised more freely recently than in any other period of our history. Protest marches, student strikes, boycotts, sit-ins, pray-ins and other forms of dissent are used by civil rights groups, labor unions, students, poor people and militant women to express dissatisfaction with things as they are.

Young people, in the forefront of current protest and dissent, have much at stake in this country. Their futures seem less and less secure. War and unrest, the army induction system, the uncertainties of dying for someone else's causes, have contributed to youth's awareness and sensitivity of the future of mankind. Senseless killings in war, growing poverty, the hateful prejudices in the world have created frustrations. College students express all this in various forms of protest.

Dissent in our country has taken on many forms. Sometimes it is expressed violently in uncontrolled anger. Campus disturbances and deaths and burned out city ghettos reflect this anger. Sometimes protest is expressed by peaceful marches, other times by well-calculated civil disobedience against what are thought to be unjust and meaningless laws.

The anguish of perpetual poverty and the anger of a prolonged war drives many people to despair. They lose faith in the system which promises them peace and security and success. In their frustration, they turn to protest and dissent. At times they go beyond the law and choose to break laws through violence.

Christians are often caught in the middle because they sense the evils that perpetuate injustices. Christians usually seek to live quiet and peaceable lives. But many wonder just how sitting back and enjoying peace and safety is going to change the injustices of society perpetuated by laws made for privileged people.

Most sensible people deplore the violence that has erupted in America as a valid recourse for expressing dissent. Actions which destroy other people's property and endanger other people's lives are obviously not in harmony with belief in the value of human life. Anarchy is wrong and senseless, but what about valid forms of civil disobedience? Or are there valid forms? Should Christians condone breaking certain laws in order to show them to be unjust? How far can a Christian dissent? Does a Christian stop at the point of civil disobedience?

In 1963, Martin Luther King demonstrated for civil rights for blacks in Birmingham, Alabama, by engaging in sit-ins and boycotts. Bull Conner, the commissioner of public safety, sought every means possible to keep Dr. King from gaining equality for black people in Birmingham. The most powerful weapon Bull

Conner had was the "law." When the Christian Southern Leadership Conference sought to dramatize the inferior status of blacks in the South by marching to the city hall of Birmingham, Bull Conner resisted with both violence (dogs and clubs) and with the "law." Conner obtained a court order for the Southern Christian Leadership Conference to cease its activities. This legal maneuver sought to delay court action until the momentum of the civil rights protest died out.

The leaders of SCLC, after careful thought and much agony of soul, decided to disobey the court injunction. They reasoned that those who would not obey a law of the Supreme Court, could not justly demand obedience to their own laws. A higher law had to be obeyed. It could not in good conscience be ignored.

Martin Luther King, in his famous "Letter from Birmingham City Jail," distinguished between two kinds of laws. He stated that there are just laws and unjust laws. A person has a moral responsbility to obey only just laws. As Augustine had said, "An unjust law is not a law at all." King did not advocate evading or defying the law as rabid segregationists would. He was against anarchy. He advocated breaking only unjust laws. He asserted that civil disobedience must be done openly, lovingly, and with a willingness to accept the consequences. In King's view, a person who breaks an unjust law which his conscience tells him is unjust, and goes to prison in order to arouse the conscience of the community against such a law, is a person with the highest respect for law. King was jailed for his actions, but later he won victories for his people by his very courage.

In these days when violence is the only method used by some dissenters, Martin Luther King's approach needs reevaluation. Physical attacks on the police, assaults on private citizens who support opposing ideas, destroying public property in protest of one cause or another, is not civil disobedience in the classical sense of the term. Those who engage in defiant lawlessness should be judged by those just laws set up to protect the citizenry.

Some Christians believe that civil disobedience is wrong and that it will inevitably lead to destruction of our society. They say the existence of our nation depends upon law and order. Lawlessness will only endanger the life of the nation. Therefore unjust laws should be changed by the traditional methods of the courts and polls, not in the streets.

What does a Christian young person do when a law becomes an instrument of seeming injustice, especially when that young person does not have the means to take a situation to court or is not old enough to vote? What does a Christian do when "law and order" is merely a way of maintaining the status quo? Can Christians support laws that openly ignore the rights of minorities? Should Christians openly violate such laws and demonstrate to build up public reaction against them? Henry David Thoreau asked, "Unjust laws exist, shall we be content to obey them or shall we endeavor to amend them at once?"

The Bible is not silent on the question of

civil disobedience. Perhaps the actions of some of God's servants have something to say to us on this urgent issue. In Acts 4, Peter and John preached the gospel and healed a lame man. Because of their preaching and the results they were having, they were brought before the religious leaders who threatened them and warned them not to preach in the name of Jesus. How they responded may be a lesson in civil disobedience for Christians.

WHAT DOES THE BIBLE SAY?

"So they called them back in and told them that under no conditions were they to speak or to teach in the name of Jesus. But Peter and John answered them: 'You yourselves judge which is right in God's sight, to obey you or to obey God. For we cannot stop speaking of what we ourselves have seen and heard. . . . And now, Lord, take notice of the threats they made and allow us, your servants, to speak your message with all boldness" (Acts 4:18-29).

"They brought the apostles in and made them stand before the Council, and the High Priest questioned them. 'We gave you strict orders not to teach in the name of this man,' he said; 'but see what you have done! You have spread your teaching all over Jerusalem, and you want to make us responsible for his death!' Peter and the other apostles answered back: 'We must obey God, not men'" (Acts 5:27-29).

"The king of Egypt also gave this order to Shiphrah and Puah, the Hebrew midwives, 'As you aid the Hebrew women in childbirth, watch them closely on the birthstool; if it is a son, kill him; if it is a daughter, let her live.' But the midwives revered God and did not carry out the orders of the king of Egypt; they kept the male babies alive. So the king of Egypt summoned the midwives and said to them, 'Why have you done this, letting the male babies live?' The midwives answered Pharaoh, 'Because Hebrew women are not like Egyptian women; they are quick of delivery, they give birth before the midwife gets to them'" (Exod. 1:15-19).

"'You, O king, have made a decree that every man who hears the sound of the horn, the pipe, the lute, the harp, the bagpipe, and every other kind of music, shall fall down and worship the golden image, and that anyone, who does not fall down and prostrate himself, shall be cast into a furnace of flaming fire. Now there are certain Jews whom you have raised to high positions . . . These three men, O king, pay no regard to you; they do not respect your gods, nor will they worship the golden image which you have set up.' Then Nebuchadrezzar was furiously enraged, and ordered Shadrach, Meshach, and Abednego to be brought . . . 'O Nebuchadrezzer, we would not make any defense in this matter; for the God whom we serve is able to save us from the fire of the furnace and He will deliver us out of your hand, O king. But, whether He does or not, be it known to you, O king, we will not serve your gods, or worship the image which you have set up'" (Dan. 3:10-18).

"So these men said, 'We shall find no ground of complaint against this Daniel unless we find it in connection with service to his god. . . . All the presidents of the kingdom, the chiefs and the governors, the counselors and the rulers have agreed that the king should establish an ordinance and enforce a strict decree, that whoever petitions any god or man for thirty days, except you, O king, shall be cast into the den of lions. . . .' When Daniel learned that such a decree had been officially signed and issued, he went to his house on the roof of which there were chambers with windows opening toward Jerusalem, and three times a day he kneeled and prayed and gave God thanks as he was accustomed to do. . . . So the king gave the order and Daniel was brought and cast into the den of lions. . . . Daniel answered the king, 'O king, live forever! My God sent His angel and shut the lions' mouths and they have not hurt me . . .'" (Dan. 6:5-22).

The Bible also has much to say about being obedient to the laws of the land:

". . . So Jesus said to them, 'Well, then, pay to the Emperor what belongs to him, and pay to God what belongs to God'" (Matt. 22:21).

"Submit yourselves, for the Lord's sake, to every human authority: to the Emperor, who is the supreme authority, and to the governors, who have been sent by him to punish the evildoers and praise those who do good. For this is God's will: he wants you to silence the ignorant talk of foolish men by the good things you do. Live as free men; do not use your freedom, however, to cover up any evil, but live as God's slaves. Respect all men, love your fellow believers, fear God, and respect the Emperor" (I Pet. 2:13-17).

"Remind your people to submit to rulers and authorities, to obey them, to be ready to do every good thing" (Titus 3:1).

"Everyone must obey the state authorities; for no authority exists without God's permission, and the existing authorities have been put there by God. Whoever opposes the existing authority opposes what God has ordered; and anyone who does so will bring judgment on himself. For rulers are not to be feared by those who do good but by those who do evil. Would you like to be unafraid of the man in authority? Then do what is good, and he will praise you. For he is God's servant working for your own good. But if you do evil, be afraid of him, for his power to punish is real. He is God's servant and carries out God's wrath on those who do evil. For this reason you must obey the authorities — not just because of God's wrath, but also as a matter of conscience. This is also the reason that you pay taxes; for the authorities are working for God when they fulfil their duties. Pay, then, what you owe them; pay them your personal and property taxes, and show respect and honor for them all" (Rom. 13:1-7).

WHAT DO YOU SAY?

1. Were the actions of Jesus in refusing to follow Sabbath laws a form of civil disobedience? In what sense?

2. Daniel 4 and 6 present definite acts of civil disobedience. Would we condemn the four Hebrews for this? Could they have taken alternate positions?

3. Is there significance in the fact that the orders to desist in Acts 4 and 5 came from religious leaders rather than from civil leaders? Did the religious leaders have civil authority?

4. Do the clear-cut examples of civil disobedience in the Bible make it an acceptable Christian approach for changing unjust laws and policies?

5. In what ways does Peter seem to contradict himself in I Peter 2 compared with his actions in Acts 4 and 5? How would you reconcile this apparent contradiction?

6. What is the difference between protest, dissent and civil disobedience? Is a public demonstration a proper and effective means of Christian protest? Why or why not?

7. If a government passed a law prohibiting door-to-door visitation on grounds that it was an invasion of privacy, would you insist that your youth group stop visiting? How would you test the validity of such a law? If it were proven constitutional, would you obey it?

8. If a law was enacted prohibiting passing out religious literature to other than churched people, would you obey it?

9. Name some unjust laws. What injustices do they protect? What can you do to change these laws?

10. Does the government under which a Christian lives determine whether civil disobedience is valid? Could you practice civil disobedience in Russia or China? How do the consequences differ from those in the United States?

11. In what circumstances can you condone Christian participation in acts of civil disobedience? Should such acts only be related to actions involving one's religious convictions?

Church Music — Does It Need Changing? 3

ARE YOU PUZZLED OR CONFUSED when you sing in church about "marching to Zion," and "bringing in the sheaves"? Have you wondered about where you could find "Beulah Land" and if you would ever see "Jordan's stormy banks"? And would you really want to "gather" at any of today's rivers?

You've probably wondered about some of the songs you sing in church. Maybe you've become so used to singing them that you never really stop to think about the words. Or perhaps you've turned them off altogether. Many adults have sung some church songs so long and so frequently that the words no longer are challenging or inspiring to them. If they would stop to think about what they are singing, they might be shocked.

You are not alone if you feel something has to be done about updating our hymnbooks. New translations of the Bible come out almost yearly, but many of the songs in our widely used hymnals are as archaic and obsolete as the wording in the King James Version of 1611. It's time to revise our hymnals by using more contemporary songs and perhaps revising some of the old favorites. Here's what can be done: new hymns could be written; new songs with contemporary styles could be included; new words could be written for the better and more lasting old tunes; new tunes could be composed for some of the better old lyrics.

Like clothing styles, music changes to reflect the mood of the times. This is as true today as it was 50 or 150 years ago. Music styles and moods are numerous. No one style of music has a monopoly on people's tastes. People listen to what suits them. Tastes may differ from day to day. Religious music, too, must develop out of the moods of the times. It has changed throughout the centuries and should continue to change.

The music produced and used in the periods of church history reflect the nature of the times. Secular forms and musical styles that have become popular have had their effects on Christian musical expression. Popular music today is having an effect on the development of new forms of sacred music. New experiments and innovations in church music are becoming popular. Some who prefer the familiar tunes and styles, however, view such changes with much misgiving. They often question the religious values of present secular forms.

The musical patterns and styles that have developed in our day have made some of our sacred music sound obsolete. Many of our gospel songs and hymns are obsolete, not only because their musical style is old, but because they no longer carry meaningful messages to modern man. Many hymns still carry a vital message and ring with majestic exuberance; these are timeless and seem never to grow old.

But those hymns that are outdated should be dropped from our hymnals to make way for new songs that incorporate the ideas and expressions of modern men. Hymns and gospel songs that only reflect the character of a past era have served their purpose and should give way to newer expressions of glory to God and witness to Jesus Christ.

With so many musical styles prevalent today, there is no agreement among Christians regarding what is suitable for Christian worship and what is not. Some deplore jazz, rock or folk music styles in Christian form. Others condemn classical and liturgical sacred music as too highbrow. Some feel that the traditional gospel choruses and gospel songs are shallow and sentimental; only chorales and stately hymns are worthy of Christian lips. While there may not be agreement among Christians about the suitability of all music for Christian worship expressions, there is a widespread acknowledgment that hymnals are overloaded with songs that no longer speak to our times, either by their lyrics or by their tunes. What is needed is an overhauling of these hymnals to include not only the best of the past but also the best of the present.

You can easily see the need for a new approach in hymnbooks by browsing through the one in your pew. You will find an overbalance of songs from the eighteenth and nineteenth centuries and a glaring neglect of the music that preceded and succeeded that time. One commonly used hymnal, published within the last ten years, does not contain one hymn by a writer born in this century. Less than 1 percent of the writers are still living.

Many of the hymns we sing do not express present day life and circumstances. Some hymns speak of being with Christ in the "garden" and being on the "Rock," and our longing for the "pearly gates." Other hymns reflect rural life and an agricultural society. What we need are hymns that speak about Christ entering lives in our fast-paced urban culture. Why can't hymns and songs be written that speak of God's presence and activity in the midst of life with speedy automobiles, computers, spacecraft, TV? Why can't we produce songs that reflect *our* needs, *our* problems and concerns, *our* circumstances? Surely we can sing of our living Lord in words and music that comes from *our* minds and hearts.

Some contemporary composers have led the way in doing something about church music. Folk songs and masses are becoming popular in some areas. Sacred jazz concerts are being scheduled. Coffeehouses are featuring the new music, and other experimental ways of using modern music forms are increasing in popularity. Most of this music has an immediate appeal to youth in youth meetings. Yet little of this type of modern music has filtered into the hymnals. For the most part, new songs are used as specials and little is being done to update congregational singing.

Let's try to put this situation into proper perspective. In other times, Christians had to adjust to new musical styles and forms. Christians during the Reformation learned to accept Luther's transformed-from-the-beer-garden tunes instead of the familiar Gregorian chants. Staid Americans had to get accustomed to the "gospel songs" that sounded like Stephen Foster minstrels — and often still do. Can Christians of today learn to listen and use the musical forms and styles that are popular today? It'll be up to youth to lead the way.

The apostle Paul told believers to encourage each other with "psalms and hymns and sacred songs" (Col. 3:16). The exact meaning of these three forms is not clear, but it is plain that Christians in the early church used a variety of forms of music in worshiping God. The periods of church history have produced a variety of church music styles. Some periods stressed congregational singing, others stressed choral and instrumental music.

Psalms used to be the accepted musical form for expressing praise and worship. The chant was popular before the Reformation and possibly went back to the times of David. Luther used popular melodies. Isaac Watts transformed congregational singing when he introduced his hymns and changed church music from psalms to singing the kind of hymns we still use today. The hymns of Watts, Wesley and other eighteenth century writers that replaced the psalm singing of their generation still stand as some of the best Christian hymns.

In the nineteenth century another style appeared — the gospel song. The gospel song stressed the personal and inner experience of the singer rather than the more worshipful formal styles of the eighteenth century. They have

31

often been labeled "I and me" songs. The revivals of the late nineteenth and early twentieth centuries produced vast numbers of gospel songs. These gospel songs dominate evangelical hymnals.

Now come the new styles and wordings. Many of them are good, many are untried, many still need to have the testing of time to prove their worth. But they need not be either looked down upon by those who would preserve all tradition, nor exalted too far above the traditional hymns. There should be a blending of the old and the new, and it will be up to young people to lead the way. The vibrant new forms need to be woven into the fabric of good presentations of the gospel and worshipful expressions to God. The challenge is yours.

WHAT DOES THE BIBLE SAY?

"Christ's message, in all its richness, must live in your hearts. Teach and instruct each other with all wisdom. Sing psalms, hymns, and sacred songs; sing to God, with thanksgiving in your hearts" (Col. 3:16).

"Speak to one another in the words of psalms, hymns, and sacred songs; sing hymns and psalms to the Lord, with praise in your hearts. Always give thanks for everything to God the Father, in the name of our Lord Jesus Christ" (Eph. 5:19, 20).

"About midnight Paul and Silas were praying and singing hymns to God, and the

other prisoners were listening to them"
(Acts 16:25).

"What should I do, then? I will pray with my spirit, but I will pray also with my mind; I will sing with my spirit, but I will sing also with my mind" (I Cor. 14:15).

"Is there any one of you who is in trouble? He should pray. Is any one happy? He should sing praises" (James 5:13).

"They sang a new song: 'You are worthy to take the scroll and to break open its seals. For you were killed, and by your death You bought men for God, From every tribe, and language, and people, and nation. You have made them a kingdom of priests to serve our God; And they shall rule the earth'" (Rev. 5:9, 10).

"O sing to the Lord a new song because He has performed wondrous things! His right hand and His holy arm have gained Him victory" (Ps. 98:1).

"Hallelujah! Sing to the Lord a new song, His praise in the congregation of the godly! Let Israel rejoice in his Maker, let the children of Zion exult in their King. Let them praise His name with processionals; let them sing praise to Him with timbrel and harp" (Ps. 149:1-3).

WHAT DO YOU SAY?

1. In what ways do our present congregational hymnbooks need to be changed? How should

hymns be revised or rewritten? Would there be any value in writing new words to some of the familiar tunes so that they would reflect more of the ideas of young people?

2. How do you determine whether a gospel song or a hymn speaks your language?

3. How do the words of the psalmist about singing a "new song" relate to using new musical forms? Why songs that are "new"?

4. What did Paul mean when he spoke about singing with the understanding? Is this a guideline for singing today? What is the purpose of singing hymns and gospel songs? Do the songs you sing in your youth group meet these purposes?

5. What does Paul's breakdown between "psalms, hymns and sacred songs" mean to youth today? Do the distinctions open the possibilities for a wide variety of musical expression for Christian worship?

6. Are there such things as "sacred" and "secular" musical styles? How do they differ?

7. Can a musical style or form be evil in itself? Is there such a thing as an immoral musical beat or tempo? If not, should all beats be brought into the church? Why not?

8. Should jazz, rock or other popular musical styles be incorporated into Christian worship? What artistic changes would be necessary?

9. Is folk rock an acceptable musical form for Christian worship? Why? Should it be used in a morning worship service or only in youth

meetings? What are the differences between folk music and Negro spirituals?

10. Should church music be chosen for its artistic and aesthetic values or for its spiritual content? What makes a song "spiritual"?

11. How can talented Christian young people be inspired to write new hymns and gospel songs? What can be done to get them accepted and incorporated into hymnbooks?

Interracial Dating — What About It? 4

YOU SUGGEST TO YOUR PARENTS or some friends that you believe in interracial dating. Troubled looks come on their faces. They accuse you of having a hang-up. You say it's their hang-up. Who's right?

The reasons behind the interracial dating hang-ups are complex and rooted deep in our history and culture. Prejudice dominates most thinking on the subject. Biblical considerations are overlooked or misrepresented and misinterpreted. Both blacks and whites have prejudiced attitudes toward the issue. The main reason for opposing interracial dating is that it leads to interracial marriage. If dating did not lead to marriage, the problem would not have so many emotional overtones. The root of the problem therefore, is really whether interracial marriage is acceptable. If society can accept such marriages, it is bound to accept the dating processes that lead to such marriages.

The question of interracial marriage is considered crucial by some because prevalent attitudes are a measure of the progress of integration. Andrew Billingsley, in his book *Black Families in White America*, points out that marriage among peoples of different racial backgrounds is considered the ultimate test of the progress of integration. It exposes caste systems that separate racial groups into superior and inferior beings. In this light, the question of interracial dating and marriage is more than a matter of personal choice; it is an index of how people are placed in national life.

The problem of interracial marriage is strong in the United States because of our long history of racial problems and misunderstandings. Interracial marriage has been forbidden by laws since the times of slavery. Not until 1967 did the Supreme Court rule against these laws.

Though there has been an increase in the number of interracial marriages during recent years, there has not been any significant change of attitudes among Americans. In a 1968 Gallup poll among fifteen thousand people in thirteen countries, the United States showed a 72 percent disapproval of marriages between whites and nonwhites — the highest of all countries polled. Only 20 percent approved; 8 percent had no opinion.

Interestingly, while public attitudes are slowly changing, evangelical Christians have generally been opposed to interracial dating and marriage. Some hold extreme views and maintain that their positions are solidly based on the Bible. One of these extreme views was expressed by a radio preacher in Dallas, Texas. According to Evangelist J. Harold Smith, "both history and the Bible reveal that any nation or people practicing intermarriage of the races soon lose both their national and racial prestige. . . . God Almighty never has, and never will, put His approval upon the marriage of different colors

. . . , as sure as that takes place, whether it is in Rome or whether it is in Greece, whether it is among the white and the black, or the white and the yellow, the yellow and the black, *that race loses its identity*. . . . God Almighty, down through these years, has preserved the races. . . . Any individul or organization in America, or any other nation, that teaches, preaches or propagates intermarriages of the races is of the *devil!*"[1] Some Scripture passages used to support the separation of the races are: Acts 17:26; Gen. 9:22; 9:24-27; Gen. 10:32; Deut. 7:1-3; Josh. 23:12, 13; Ezra 9:12; and Deut. 22:9-11.

The question, of course, concerning these and other Scriptures is whether they have reference to intermarriage based on race or on faith. The purity demanded by God was a moral and spiritual one. His command to avoid intermarriage with foreigners was a prohibition against polluting their lives with pagan practices. A careful study of these Scriptures will show this is the primary meaning. To make these passages refer to purity of race seems a gross misinterpretation and misunderstanding of what the Bible teaches.

Many of the reasons given for opposing marriage between the races are based on the bad sociological and psychological effects these marriages are supposed to produce. Opponents of intermarriage often question the motives of people who decide to date or marry a person of another race. Friendship or love is often denied as being the real reason.

Many people are bound by common stereotypes that are rooted in prejudice and fear. One stereotype holds that the white girl who marries a Negro must be morally depraved and oversexed because a *normal* white woman couldn't bear the average male Negro's savage sexual power. And the white man who marries a Negro woman will soon tire of her extraordinary sensuality and return to the safer and saner practices of his own kind. No one has ever scientifically validated these claims of sexual incompatability between the races. These ideas are only assumptions held by those who are prejudiced against a particular race, usually against Negroes.

The stereotypes, in any particular case, may or may not have validity. No one can fully judge the individual reasons and the complex factors that go into personal relationships between two people, regardless of race. Perhaps society should not be asking what motivates people to intermarry, rather they should be asking themselves why they seek to know. Can we honestly treat people as humans and continue asking such questions? Aren't the questions themselves often motivated by prejudice and traces of racism deeply rooted in our lives?

Many will not accept interracial couples, whether those who date or those who marry. The hostility of prejudiced people is one argument used against intermarriage. People ask, "What will happen to your children?" "What will your friends think?" "What will your parents say?" "What about your children's children?" Questions like these are not fully valid or reasonable, nevertheless they are continually asked.

Hilda Bryant, writing in *Christian Life Magazine*,[2] asked whether a Christian Caucasian could marry a Christian Negro and expect a successful marriage by scriptural standards. One of the couples she interviewed (Marna and Ed Matthews), both highly dedicated and intelligent Christians, found little discrimination that bothered them. Ed summed up his view this way, "I see as my purpose letting people know that Christ is the most important Person to me and that He feels that I am important to Him no matter what race I am. . . . Our marriage is based on the teaching of Christ, and I think this is a foundation strong enough. My education helps — it helps to be able to go to work every day, to have a definite income and not worry about getting fired. I think there would be more hang-ups with a Catholic-Protestant marriage than with an interracial one." Mrs. Bryant concluded that the answer to the question, "Can a Christian interracial marriage be successful by scriptural standards?" must be "Yes."

Studies of interracially married couples have shown that they have the normal problems of husband-wife relations, but there have been no evidences of sexual incompatabilities. The studies have revealed a certain amount of prejudice against both parents and children, but the discrimination is not so much against the marriage itself as it is against the Negro partner.

Christian young people must come to grips with the question of interracial dating and marriage for at least two reasons. First, because it is a moral and spiritual question. Reasons for or against may be motivated by prejudice or fear rather than conviction and facts. Opposition on the basis of racial pride or prejudice is not Christian. Young people must ask whether their attitudes are motivated by fear, prejudice or Christian love.

The second reason Christian young people need to face this question is that they are interacting in interracial situations more frequently. High schools and colleges are more interracially mixed. The opportunities for developing friendships with people of other races are more frequent. It is inevitable that people who share the same classroom, who eat in the same lunchroom, and who go to the same church, will be attracted to other people, regardless of race. As young people and adults see people as human beings, the barriers of race will mean less and less. Consequently the thought that something is wrong with dating a black or white or yellow will not even come up. How will you react when you see one of your friends dating a person of another race? Will you criticize? Will you whisper? Or will you accept it as natural and acceptable? Are you yourself prepared for falling in love with a person of another race? It's possible, isn't it?

WHAT DOES THE BIBLE SAY?

"And I will have you swear by the Lord, the God of heaven and earth, that you will not get my son a wife from the daughters of the Canaanites, among whom I am living" (Gen. 24:3).

"Isaac then called Jacob and blessed him; he also charged him, 'You are to marry no Canaanite girl'" (Gen. 28:1).

"When a stranger lives among you in your land, do not maltreat him; the foreigner who lives among you shall be like a native among you. You shall love him as your own, because you were strangers in the land of Egypt . . ." (Lev. 19:33, 34).

"When the Most High gave the nations their heritage, when He separated the sons of men, He set the boundaries of the peoples in accord with the number of the sons of Israel" (Deut. 32:8).

". . . The land which you are about to possess is unclean due to the wicked practices of the people of the land, as they have filled it from one end to the other with their abominations. Therefore, let there be no intermarrying between your daughters and their sons or their daughters and your sons, and never further their peace or their prosperity, that you may be strong and eat the good of the land and leave it for an inheritance for your children forever" (Ezra 9: 11, 12).

"Have we not all one Father? Has not one God created us? Why are we faithless to one another, profaning the covenant of our fathers?" (Mal. 2:10).

43

" '. . . For this reason a man will leave his father and mother and unite with his wife, and the two shall become one.' So they are no longer two, but one. Man must not separate, then, what God has joined together" (Matt. 19:5, 6).

"From the one man he created all races of men, and made them live over the whole earth . . ." (Acts 17:26).

"So there is no difference between Jews and Gentiles, between slaves and free men, between men and women: you are all one in union with Christ Jesus" (Gal. 3:28).

"My brothers! In your life as believers in our Lord Jesus Christ, the Lord of glory, you must never treat people in different ways because of their outward appearance. . . . But if you treat people according to their outward appearance, you are guilty of sin, and the Law condemns you as a lawbreaker" (James 2:1-9).

WHAT DO YOU SAY?

1. What is the main reason young people of different races decide to date one another? What would motivate you personally to practice interracial dating? Do you think the increase in such dating is good or bad?

2. Should young people avoid interracial dating since it may lead to marriage and consequent hostility from parents and friends?

3. Are there any biological reasons for pro-

hibiting marriage between the races? Is there such a thing as a "pure" race?

4. Why do people question the motives of those who want to intermarry? Is such questioning right and fair? Why shouldn't everybody who wants to marry be subject to the same type of questions and doubt?

5. Why is the question of interracial marriage so vital to the progress of integration? Can there be true integration without intermarriage?

6. If two Christians of different races love each other and are "one in Christ," are there any biblical or other reasons why such a marriage shouldn't take place? Are there any grounds for separating the races by prohibiting intermarriage?

7. Are the Old Testament warnings to the Jews against marrying non-Israelites valid references to use against present day interracial marriages? Do they have reference to purity of race or purity of faith?

8. Can the practice of applying Scripture against interracial marriage become a form of prejudice or racism? Explain. Does the Bible condone racism in any form?

Notes

[1]J. Harold Smith, "God's Plan for the Races, America's Number One Problem, Segregation," Radio Bible Hour, Dallas, Texas.

[2]Hilda Bryant, "Interracial Marriage," *Christian Life*, January 1969. Used by permission of Christian Life Publications, Inc. Gundersen Drive and Schmale Road, Wheaton, Illinois 60187.

Use Drugs? 5

IF SOMEONE IN YOUR FAMILY was involved in an auto accident and was in severe pain at the hospital, you'd want a doctor to administer a modern pain reliever. If someone else you love had emotional problems that needed tranquilizers to calm his anxieties, you'd be happy if such pills were available. When you get Headache No. 32, you're glad for the Excedrin bottle. If you have a cough and a cold, a dose of cough liquid is a great relief.

Modern drugs and the science of pharmacology have done wonders for the relief of illness and pain. Drugs are a vital part of modern life. Millions of people would suffer needlessly if we did not have a vast knowledge of drugs that kill pain or help rehabilitate diseased tissue. You probably wouldn't want to live in a world that had no pain relievers or wonder drugs.

While modern drugs are some of the most beneficial products manufactured, many of them have become man's enemies through abuse. Drugs can become powerful destroyers of mind and body.

There's no denying that some drugs bend your mind, put you into hallucinogenic states, give you a drunk, make you feel like a floating ball. But in the process the person's mind can become severely damaged. A few trips just aren't worth a lifetime of mental anguish or deterioration.

It's true, some people even get hooked on drugs prescribed by doctors. They get "turned on" in the doctor's office. Many doctors are aware of the potential problems, yet they prescribe drugs that are dangerous. The problems of life are escaped for a short time, but when the drugs wear off, the problems return. Swallowing mind-bending pills to avoid reality is a poor way to go through life. Sooner or later the reality appears as it is.

The use of mind-altering drugs is widespread. The *New York Times* estimates that over one hundred million Americans use alcohol, amphetamines, barbiturates, and tranquilizers. About 20 percent of the prescriptions filled in the country are for mind altering drugs. These drugs include those which can be purchased without prescriptions. Anyone who habitually uses drugs has a potential drug problem. Those who can't do without drugs are labeled addicts.

The World Health Organization defines drug addiction as "a state of periodic or chronic intoxication produced by the repeated consumption of a drug (natural or synthetic). The characteristics of addiction include: 1) an uncontrollable desire and need to continue taking a drug and to get it by any means; 2) a tendency to increase the dosage; 2) a psychological and physical dependence on the effects of the drug; 4) a detrimental effect on the addict and on society."

The Royal Bank of Canada's Newsletter stated: "Drugs are used by people who feel small in the face of the complexities of life, by people who seek a temporary feeling of importance, by people who wish to depress their anxiety or to raise their spirits, or by people who desire to experience hallucinations. It is this unnatural self-indulgence that is the damaging use of drugs."[1]

Drugs produce a variety of effects. Caffeine, cocaine, and amphetamines combat fatigue. Alcohol, barbiturates, and morphine banish worries and induce sleep. Marijuana, mescaline and lysergic acid (LSD) cause dreams.

Adults are becoming alarmed about the excessive use of illegal drugs. Research has found that many get hooked through ignorance. Other factors contributing to drug abuse are: the temper of the times, the breakdown of the family, social unrest, the threat of annihilation, youthful independence and rebellion. Unfortunately, many young people do not look at drug abuse as a moral problem. They forget that every person has a moral responsibility to himself, to society and to his Creator.

David Wilkerson, who has worked with drug addicts for many years in his Teen Challenge centers, takes strong issue with those who say drugs aren't harmful. He disagrees totally with the current permissive attitude toward marijuana. "I consider marijuana the most dangerous drug used today," he dogmatically states. "What the experts, who think they know all the answers, don't know or say is this: *90 percent of all the drug addicts we have ever treated began with marijuana and then graduated to something harder.*"2

Wilkerson has had enough firsthand experience with marijuana users to flatly state that they get as hooked on pot as persons addicted to heroin. He's dealt with chronic marijuana users who've lost their motivation and developed antisocial tendencies which led to violent antisocial acts.

"I know what marijuana does," he states. "It breaks down resistance to drugs. It paves the way to alcoholism and drug addiction. It destroys moral values, especially sex standards."

Dr. James L. Goddard, former director of the U.S. Food and Drug Administration, believes that those who argue for the legalization of marijuana simply ignore the ill effects of the drug upon the user. Some say that its use is private, that it is less harmful than alcohol. Dr. Goddard says, "If the known harmful effects of alcohol and tobacco are greater than those of marijuana, and those substances are legal, why do I not advocate legalizing marijuana? I believe that if alcohol and tobacco were not already legal, we might very well decide not to legalize them — knowing what we know now."3 One only has to review the statistics of highway deaths caused by drunkenness to see how dangerous a drug can be. Could society bear another problem as serious as alcohol has become?

Lambert Dolphin, who experimented with LSD before he became a Christian, tells about his trips: "Shortly after taking LSD, music became ecstatically alive and full of living richness. Vivid color patterns and phantasies in three dimensions filled my mind when I closed my eyes. With my eyes open, objects in the room took on amazing shapes and shimmering glows. Gradually I lost my awareness of my body. Strange emotional experiences and long-forgotten dreams bubbled up inside. I felt outside of myself, looking from a new perspective into thousands of corridors of my life. Time became strangely distorted and I experienced the terrible sensation of time stoppage and endless eternity. Unpleasant and terrible fears associated with conception, birth, and early childhood gripped my mind for painfully long periods of time. I was caught up in closed cycles of temporary insanity and terrible vast worlds of unreality."[4]

Christian youth must learn what the Bible says about keeping a clear mind and facing life depending on God rather than upon drugs. It takes no spiritual commitment to experience mind-bending and high experiences with drugs, but the Christian's mind must be transformed and conformed to the image of Jesus Christ. Because God offers abundant life in Christ, there is no need for substitutes. Christ can fill any void that modern life may bring. True mind expansion comes through experiencing the mind of Christ, not through drugging oneself senseless. Drugs destroy the mind. Strong and vibrant minds do not need drugs to find fulfillment and happiness. It is the weak that demand substitutes.

The Bible speaks of being controlled by the Spirit. Drunkenness is condemned because it renders a person incapable of making sound judgments. Drugs which alter a person's sensibilities and cause a person to lose control of his mental and spiritual abilities are not the means by which a Christian can find peace or happiness. The Christian who is controlled by the Spirit of God and who has yielded himself to God has experienced a "high" that no drug could ever produce. And the aftereffects won't put you into a mental ward or behind prison bars.

WHAT DOES THE BIBLE SAY?

"Happy are those whose greatest desire is to do what God requires: God will satisfy them fully!" (Matt. 5:6).

". . . Do not be worried about the food and drink you need to stay alive, or about clothes for your body. After all, isn't life worth more than food? and isn't the body worth more than clothes?" (Matt. 6:25).

"Let them give thanks to the Lord for His mercy and for His wonderful deeds to the children of men! For He satisfies the thirsty soul and provides the hungry with good" (Ps. 107:8, 9).

"Don't worry about anything, but in all your prayers ask God for what you need, always asking him with a thankful heart. And God's peace, which is far beyond human understanding, will keep your hearts and minds safe, in Christ Jesus" (Phil. 4: 6, 7).

"There they offered him wine to drink,

mixed with gall; after tasting it, however, he would not drink it" (Matt. 27:34).

". . . I have come in order that they might have life, life in all its fullness" (John 10:10).

"Jesus answered: 'Whoever drinks this water will get thirsty again; but whoever drinks the water that I will give him will never be thirsty again. For the water that I will give him will become in him a spring which will provide him with living water, and give him eternal life'" (John 4:13, 14).

"So then, my brothers, because of God's many mercies to us, I make this appeal to you: Offer yourselves a living sacrifice to God, dedicated to his service and pleasing to him. This is the true worship that you should offer. Do not conform outwardly to the standards of this world, but let God transform you inwardly by a complete change of your mind. Then you will be able to know the will of God — what is good, and is pleasing to him, and is perfect" (Rom. 12:1, 2).

"Someone will say, 'I am allowed to do anything.' Yes; but not everything is good for you. I could say, 'I am allowed to do anything'; but I am not going to let anything make a slave of me" (I Cor. 6:12).

"Don't you know that your body is the temple of the Holy Spirit, who lives in you, the Spirit given you by God? You do not belong to yourselves but to God; he bought you for a price. So use your bodies for God's glory" (I Cor. 6:19, 20).

WHAT DO YOU SAY?

1. What are the factors in modern living that have made the use of drugs so widespread among youth? Are any of these reasons legitimate? Why or why not?

2. Why do drugs like marijuana have such a strong appeal? Does education about harmful effects curb drug usage? Why or why not?

3. Is the argument that marijuana isn't any worse than alcohol a valid argument? What are some of the effects of alcohol? In what ways are the effects of marijuana similar to alcohol? If marijuana is as bad as alcohol, isn't that reason enough not to use it?

4. Since drugs keep people from facing the realities of life, is this adequate reason not to use them? In what ways are drugs poor substitutes for facing life's problems?

5. What should be the Christian's attitude toward using tranquilizers and barbiturates to relieve tensions and to produce sleep?

6. Should amphetamines, barbiturates, LSD and other drugs ever be taken without a doctor's advice? Why or why not? What are some serious dangers of LSD?

7. Can aspirin and other pain relievers be harmful? What is the difference between using aspirin to relieve a headache and taking marijuana to feel high?

8. Although marijuana isn't habit forming, almost all users of hard narcotics began with pot. Shouldn't the threat of becoming a narcotic addict keep one from using marijuana? Why doesn't it?

9. What in the Christian message implies that drug taking is a poor and needless substitute for a personal experience with Jesus Christ? In view of this truth, do Christians ever need to indulge in drug usage other than for therapeutic reasons?

10. For what reasons, if any, should Christians use drugs? Should certain drugs be avoided? Why?

11. What can Christian youth do to lead drug abusers away from the illegal and dangerous use of drugs? What are you doing in your school and community?

12. If a personal friend is selling or using drugs illegally, do you have a moral and legal responsibility to inform law enforcement officials?

Notes

[1]"Misuse of Drugs: Some Facts," *The Royal Bank of Canada Monthly Letter*, September 1968. Used by permission.

[2]David Wilkerson, "Should Marijuana Be Legalized?" *The Church Herald*, March 15, 1968. Used by permission.

[3]James L. Goddard, "Should It Be Legalized? 'Soon We Will Know,'" *Life*, October 31, 1969. Used by permission.

[4]Lambert Dolphin, Jr., "A Trip with LSD," *His*, March 1967. Reprinted by permission from *His*, student magazine of Inter-Varsity Christian Fellowship, © 1967.

Should Youth Give Up the Church? 6

You don't need a church building to have a church. You don't need a preacher to study the Bible. You don't need organization to worship God. Young people are seriously considering these ideas and have often drawn the conclusion that they don't need what is called "the institutional church." In fact, some look at the institutional church as a definite hindrance to the work of God in the world. They can name churches that have turned down youth-oriented programs. They can name churches that have done little to benefit their communities. They point out that hundreds of resolutions have been passed in church conventions concerning social changes while few people who return from such gatherings fulfill the resolutions. Thus they conclude that the institutional church doesn't want to change. Some have given up on the church because they look upon it as a dead entity where commitment of their energies and ideas would be a lost cause.

Statistics show that the church is losing its influence in our society. In 1969 a Gallup poll reported "one of the most dramatic reverses of opinion in the history of polling." In 1957, only 14 percent of all persons polled said that religion was losing influence. In 1969, 70 percent said it was losing ground. This change in opinion parallels the decline in churchgoing in America. The decline is most dramatic among young people. While the national church attendance declined six points since 1958, the drop was nearly 15 percent among young adults and collegians.

Reasons for believing the church is losing ground included such answers as: "The church says nothing about social issues." "Morals have changed but the church preaches Victorian ethics." "The church is mostly a middle class institution unconcerned about the matters of poverty and race." "While preaching against materialism, the church has become rich in property and business enterprises." "The church is more interested in property rights than in human rights." "The older generation is afraid of a take-over by the youth."

It has become popular on college campuses for professors to use the church as a scapegoat for many of the country's social ills. Even television commentators and interviewers have taken a cynical attitude when interviewing church leaders or examining church programs. It seems to be the "in" thing for young people to join the attack on the church — even though they have grown up in the church.

Many church critics see the church as outmoded, disinterested, and a decaying institution that has lost its usefulness and meaning in modern society. The church is seen as a self-serving organization that cares about its own status rather than about the critical problems of the world. It is bent on preserving its own traditions and cultic practices rather than relating itself to the needs of modern man in a changing technological age.

These critics say that drastic renewal is needed — even to the destruction of present forms and structures. Some would abandon the church altogether and do away with all tradition. "Let's begin anew," they say — usually with few constructive alternatives to offer. Some suggest that the church should be radically changed by using nonreligious terms, forms, and content. They have reacted to the otherworldliness and exclusiveness of some Christians. They claim that the world isn't listening to much of the conservatives' jargon about heaven and how to get there, and so a totally new language needs to be developed that is centered primarily in social betterment. Religious issues must give way to racial problems; social answers must have primary importance over soul needs; poverty outbids piety; confrontation outshines conversion. Religion, for these critics, must become totally involved in the secular society.

Criticism of today's church isn't limited to Protestantism. The Roman Catholic Church is being rocked by dissent. Underground churches meet apart from the organized structure; celebrate their own masses, have informal discussions, and pay little attention to the dictums of the hierarchy. In many cases, priests and nuns are the vanguard of the underground movements.

There is another, perhaps more healthy, concern being shown over the faults of the church. There are those who are deeply concerned about the ills of the church, but as a doctor diagnosing sickness in a human body, they are not ready to kill the body of the church just to rid it of some ills.

Many evangelicals are greatly disturbed about the problems the church faces. They see the irrelevancy, social unconcern, the suburban syndrome, the culture gaps, the unlistening world and ask themselves what they can do. Some start new churches only to find that people are the same everywhere and that new organizations inherit the problems of the old. Others stay within the context of their local churches seeking to renew and revive their ministries. Cell groups and neighborhood Bible study groups are developing throughout the country. These are putting new life into churches and challenging traditional methods of church ministry.

In 1968, a group of evangelical young men, formerly staff members of Campus Crusade for Christ, drew up plans for establishing "first-century churches." The group called itself "Acts 29" and started churches in homes and colleges, free from expensive buildings, complex programs, full-time pastors and organizational machinery. The group, made up of Christian activists who call for a reformation in the contemporary church, advocate a first-century type church. This movement seeks this either within or without the "organized ecclesiastical establishment."

Most evangelicals do not accept the radical notions that the idea of the church be scrapped and that we do away with church buildings, formal ministries, Sunday schools, and weekly religious services on Sunday. They recognize that the church has weaknesses, but believe that changes should be made within the context of present structures. They do not blindly accept the idea that the church is decadent and irrelevant. Christ is still shared and proclaimed through the church. The local church is still the focal point of the work of God in the world. Too much of the criticism aimed at the church is misdirected, grossly unfair, and is being made by those who have not entered into the ministries the church is performing in the world.

While the church is undergoing severe criticism, it is still a strong and meaningful organism in society. One measure of its life is its missionary outreach. The number of foreign missionaries is at an all-time high. Nearly thirty-five thousand Protestant missionaries seek to bring the social, as well as the spiritual, benefits of the gospel to millions of people around the world. Much of present missionary work concerns itself with the physical, educational and social benefits to people. Here at home, there are outreaches into ghettos, hippie settlements and college campuses. Inter-Varsity Christian Fellowship and Campus Crusade for Christ are making dramatic inroads into college campuses by winning hundreds of young people to Christ.

Many local churches have taken on new vitality. They are reaching their communities with socially related programs as well as with the soul-changing gospel. While they remain vitally concerned with man's spiritual development, they recognize that spiritual maturity is a highly necessary part of human development. Many young people are finding within the church a challenging opportunity to accomplish both spiritual and social goals. They have found that criticism of the church alone is not the answer. It also involves self-examination. Someone has challenged the church critics with this quip: "What's wrong with the church may be you — and me!" Possibly that's where we all (young and old) need to begin before we decide to give up on the church.

WHAT DOES THE BIBLE SAY?

". . . and on this rock I will build my church. Not even death will ever be able to overcome it" (Matt. 16:18).

"For where two or three come together in my name, I am there with them" (Matt. 18:20).

"Jesus said to her: 'Believe me, woman, the time will come when men will not worship the Father either on this mountain or in Jerusalem. . . . But the time is coming, and is already here, when the real worshipers will worship the Father in spirit and in truth. These are the worshipers the Father wants to worship him'" (John 4:21-23).

"Live in such a way as to cause no trouble either to Jews, or Gentiles, or to the church of God" (I Cor. 10:32).

"Everything must be done in a proper and orderly way" (I Cor. 14:40).

"God put all things under Christ's feet, and

gave him to the church as supreme Lord over all things. The church is Christ's body, the completion of him who himself completes all things everywhere" (Eph. 1:22, 23).

"So then, you Gentiles are not foreigners or strangers any longer, you are now fellow-citizens with God's people, and members of the family of God! You, too, are built upon the foundation laid by the apostles and prophets, the cornerstone being Christ Jesus himself. He is the one who holds the whole building together and makes it grow into a sacred temple in the Lord. In union with him you too are being built together with all the others into a house where God lives through his Spirit" (Eph. 2:19-22).

"He is the head of his body, the church; he is the source of the body's life; he is the first-born Son who was raised from death . . ." (Col. 1:18, see Col. 2:18, 19).

"But if I delay, this letter will let you know how we should conduct ourselves in God's household, which is the church of the living God, the pillar and support of the truth" (I Tim. 3:15).

"I know what you have done; I know that you are neither cold nor hot. How I wish you were either one or the other! But because you are barely warm, neither hot nor cold, I am about to spit you out of my mouth! 'I am rich and well off,' you say, 'I have all I need.' But you do not know how

63

miserable and pitiful you are! You are poor, naked, and blind" (Rev. 3:15-17).

WHAT DO YOU SAY?

1. Define what you mean by the institutional church. Does your local church come under this definition? Is that good or bad? Why or why not?

2. Was the first-century church an "institutional" church? Is the church of the New Testament era an adequate model for us? What elements of early church practice would not fit into twentieth-century Christianity?

3. To what was Jesus referring when He said, "I will build my church"? Was He speaking about an organization? Was the matter of organizational structure a New Testament concern?

4. If you were to restructure the church, what kind of organization would you have? Be specific. What guarantees would you have that the new structure would not have many of the problems of the present church?

5. Some have tried the coffeehouse approach for expressing Christian worship and witness. Are there any weaknesses in this approach? What are its strengths?

6. What present day attacks on the church do you consider valid? What alternatives to present approaches do you suggest? How would you implement these approaches?

7. In what ways must church youth share in the criticisms made of the church?

8. What type of positive ministries are you en-

gaged in? How do you propose to make your church more relevant in your community?

9. What are some of the dangers young people face in rejecting the traditional approaches to Christian worship and work? What should be done to keep new approaches biblically based?

10. Since young people will be the leaders of the church in the next decade, what are you personally doing to develop the qualities of leadership that will spread and maintain the dynamic of the gospel in our culture?

Time on Your Hands! 7

YOUR MOTHER ASKED, "Where are you going?" You answered, "No place in particular. Probably downtown for a ride." And that's exactly what you did. You had an evening to kill so you and a couple of friends killed it — riding around block after block; sipping Cokes at a snack restaurant; chatting about things you would hardly remember the next day; standing on the corner watching cars go round and round the same block.

Leisure has been called one of the modern dangers facing Western civilization. People seem quite unprepared to cope with the prospect of having more time on their hands. Too often the only reaction is to fill time with meaningless activities, just once more around the block.

As long as a person keeps occupied, what's the difference what he does with his time? Why should I worry about what others do with their time? Isn't that an individual decision? Who can evaluate the importance of another's activities? Is he or she wasting time? By what standards do we judge the value of time? All these questions seem legitimate on the surface, but often they are asked because a person hasn't developed a satisfactory approach toward using his own time. Having too much free time often leads to idleness and its twin sister — laziness. Its cousin, aimlessness, creeps into a person's life and not only dulls daily living but threatens one's career.

In the past sixty years, Americans have reduced the average work week from seventy to less than forty working hours. Yet people today seem to have less leisure than their forefathers. Modern conveniences have freed many from long working hours, but many of these free people fritter away the leisure hours they've gained. They spend a lot of time driving on congested highways, commuting on crowded suburban trains, waiting in grocery stores, watching meaningless or mediocre TV programs, putting gadgets on their automobiles. Probably most of us have kicked ourselves after an evening's indulgence in some second-rate TV movie. Why did we waste that time?

Having more goods and services available hasn't really given the average person more time to relax or to enjoy life. Many spend their extra hours seeking to discover activities to cure their boredom. Others find a second job in order to pay for all the timesaving devices they have purchased. Too many of us, regardless of our economic level, are caught in and often contribute much to the ongoing of the "rat race." We've become slaves to our possessions and activities.

What should you do with your time? Is it merely something to be filled with activities? Some men look upon time in terms of quantity — so many hours in which to do a specific number of things. Have you ever told your parents that you couldn't stay home because you had nothing to do at home? You couldn't stand not being in some busy activity. You couldn't stand silence. You needed action. Few of us take the qualitative look at time — what significant, beneficial, rewarding and constructive things can we do? We are too busy keeping our wheels spinning to do much qualitative thinking about our time.

The key word to describe the American use of leisure is "activity." We have to be doing something all the time. In fact, we spend over $80 billion every year in leisure time activities — travel, entertainment, sports, games, etc. In our affluent society, leisure is defined mostly as pleasure. Our chief aim is to live it up! This is true whether you are part of the now generation or the older generation.

It is not wrong to have fun. The natural fruit of good living is the enjoyment of life. (See Eccl. 2:24-26 and I Cor. 3:21-23.) Yet the Christian has a responsibility beyond momentary enjoyment. His attitude toward leisure and pleasure goes beyond the "live it up" philosophy. Leisure, as Webster defines it, is "freedom to do something." The Christian believes that time is a stewardship in much the same manner as he considers his talents and money as a stewardship to God. A Christian's time is never separated from his faith. Every moment, including those in which he is enjoying himself to the fullest, is lived in the context of the Spirit's control.

Does this mean that God is a killjoy? On the contrary, He has given us many pursuits and activities to enjoy. He has given us creative imagination to make our work more efficient and our pleasure more enjoyable. He tells us that whatever we do, we should do it heartily (Col. 3:23). The apostle Paul told the Colossians that whatever they were to do, whether in word or in deed, they were to do all in the name of the Lord Jesus, thanking God the Father (Col. 3:17). Surely pleasurable leisure is a God-given enjoyment that can be done in the name of the Lord Jesus. The abundant life doesn't mean that every minute is taken up with something religious. God gave us the world to enjoy. If we keep the rules He set down there's no reason why we can't enjoy the best of what He has provided for us.

Unfortunately there are some young people who put their religion in the leisure category. They make it an elective, a spare time activity like going to a football game or bird watching. But according to the New Testament, religion is a full time activity. You can't be a part-timer in Christianity. A Christian is never off duty for God.

One great New Testament phrase about time is "redeeming the time" (Eph. 5:16; Col. 4:5). This means literally to "buy back time" in the sense that time has been taken away from us and therefore we should do everything possible to get it back, to redeem it. Our Lord gave us the best example. He was a wise steward of His time. He used His hours to the greatest advantage. This does not mean that He never enjoyed Himself. A careful study of the gospels shows that He had many enjoyable, entertaining and exciting encounters with others. We do well to study His use of time and pattern our lives after His.

A common misconception among Christians is that they must always be working. Many fill up their spare time with only church-related activities. Some look upon recreation as of little spiritual value and some even consider it evil. Some Christians hold down two jobs and work up to sixteen hours a day, driving themselves constantly because they don't want to sit around or because they are afraid to take out leisure time. Eventually they enslave themselves either to money or to work. Psychologists have classified these people as work addicts. These kinds of people often fall victims to what preachers used to call the "barrenness of a busy life."

Leisure, for the Christian, does not mean left-over time; it is too important and too serious to be regarded lightly. But it does not follow that filling one's time at a maddening clip is redeeming the time.

What will you do with leisure time as it increases? Will the freedom from endless labor release you from the insecurities and fears that now plague mankind? Will you know how to use your leisure to pursue peace and goodness? Will you use it for selfish reasons and self-indulgence, or will you use it for helping others? Will you use it to promote harmony between people or to separate them from one another?

In the future people will continue to pursue leisure in two ways — by pleasure or by service. Can you keep the two in balance? Can you avoid becoming addicted to the "pleasure first" philosophy and demonstrate that life can be enjoyed in many ways, like ways that involve helping eliminate poverty, caring for the sick and the aged, reducing crime, rehabilitating alcoholics and addicts, and sharing Christ with the world? It would be a pity if our only response to the pressing needs of society was "I don't have time."

WHAT DOES THE BIBLE SAY?

"On the seventh day God ended His work which He had been doing; He rested on the seventh day from all the works He had accomplished" (Gen. 2:2).

"My times are in Thy hand; free me from my foes, and from my pursuers" (Ps. 31:15).

"He makes me to lie down in green pastures; He leads me beside restful waters; He revives my soul . . ." (Ps. 23:2-3).

"But the wicked are like the troubled sea; it cannot rest and its waters cast up mire and dirt. There is no peace, says my God, for the wicked" (Isa. 57:20, 21).

"Come to me, all of you who are tired from carrying your heavy loads, and I will give you rest. Take my yoke and put it on you, and learn from me, for I am gentle and humble in spirit; and you will find rest" (Matt. 11:28, 29).

". . . So he said to them, 'Let us go off by ourselves to some place where we will be

72

alone and you can rest a while'" (Mark 6: 31).

"The Lord answered her, 'Martha, Martha! You are worried and troubled over so many things, but just one is needed. Mary has chosen the right thing, and it will not be taken away from her'" (Luke 10: 41, 42).

"Then I will say to myself: Lucky man! You have all the good things you need for many years. Take life easy, eat, drink, and enjoy yourself! But God said to him, 'You fool! This very night you will have to give up your life; then who will get all these things you have kept for yourself?'" (Luke 12:19-20).

"So pay close attention to how you live. Don't live like ignorant men, but like wise men. Make good use of every opportunity you get, because these are bad days. Don't be fools, then, but try to find out what the Lord wants you to do" (Eph. 5:15-17).

"Be wise in the way you act toward those who are not believers, making good use of every opportunity you have" (Col. 4:5).

WHAT DO YOU SAY?

1. What is leisure? Is it the absence of work? Can work ever be leisure? Does it always have to include pleasure or rest? How does leisure differ from laziness and idleness?

2. In what ways is modern man unprepared for increased leisure time? Why has more free time caused boredom among many young people? How does boredom relate to a person's inner life? Can boredom produce antisocial behavior? How?

3. Why do many Christians believe you have to be working at something most of the time? Do the Christians you know enjoy their leisure time? Why or why not?

4. What are the dangers of constant activity without taking out time for rest or relaxation? What are the dangers of too much leisure?

5. Has additional leisure time been detrimental or helpful to the youth programs in your church?

6. How much should Sundays be used for family and personal leisure activities? By what criteria do you measure or determine how you use your Sundays?

7. Would three-day weekends give Christians more time for church related activities? How could churches change their programs if we had a nationwide four-day workweek? Would you give more of your time to the church? How?

8. Give some examples of good uses of leisure time. What are some bad uses? What makes one thing more acceptable than another?

9. How should Christians use their vacation time? How can vacations become more profitable — spiritually, mentally and physically?

10. How did Jesus and His disciples use their

leisure time? What biblical principles can we learn from their actions? How did Jesus' attitude toward the Sabbath differ from those of the religious leaders? Are there any modern counterparts?

Who's Widening the Generation Gap? 8

THERE HAVE ALWAYS BEEN CONFLICTS between young people and adults. The talk about youth being rebellious is older than the now generation. At one time today's adults rebelled in many ways against their parents. But modern technology dramatizes the tensions between the young and the old. The present estrangement and alienation between the generations seems to go deeper than the ordinary rebellion of youth. Why? A larger portion of the population falls in the "under-twenty-five" category. The sheer numbers of the now generation help to produce conflicts and tensions.

Today's young people have the means to broadcast their views and therefore they can make their demands known much better than youth of any previous generation. The "gap" has taken on such proportions that it has become a household word and perhaps has become a scapegoat for many of our nation's problems. The gap cannot be overlooked. Youth as well as adults have to look at it and do something constructive about eliminating it.

Perhaps the generation gap has been widened by the swift pace of our times. Technology and automation have made possible the ability to create a world with fantastic possibilities for either good or evil. Instant communication tells us of the horrors of war, spectacular space adventures, the increase in our standards of living, the desperate needs of much of the world's population — and the unconcern of many who seem bent on living for the dollar and what it will provide in this world's comforts. And since the adult generation has had more experience in the money game, the younger generation can criticize more.

But the horizons of today's youth are wider and they become sophisticated earlier in life. They are more aware of the environment and sensitive to its needs. It is a TV-oriented generation that is accustomed to immediate presentation and response to the news. Youth have been deluged with information and are constantly confronted with the cynical truths of life at an early age — perhaps too soon and without proper experience to adequately evaluate the issues. The now people are impatient with the snail's pace of much of the older generation. They want action and want it immediately. They rebel when they are told to wait. Generations that receive whatever they desire cannot easily be taught to follow the virtue of patience.

As in other generations, youth today are idealistic. They are strong in tolerance, justice, equality, civil rights, freedom and peace. They are impatient with the inconsistencies and moral hypocrisy of the older generation. They question tradition and authority and do not accept the ideas arbitrarily forced on them.

The generation gap has produced a conflict of authority and values. You have a different set of values than your parents. You have been taught to be discerning and are quick to see that sometimes your parents or others of the older generation don't practice what they preach. You can quickly detect dishonesty and double standards. You are impatient with hypocrisy and sham. You are less concerned about success and security and more concerned about human values, even if you have difficulty explaining what you mean by "human values."

It's easy to label the burden you have about the value system of the older generation. Just label it "the system" and "the establishment." It's with this "establishment" that most young people have their greatest authority conflict. Parents, teachers and political leaders are part of that system and therefore are suspect.

It has been difficult for the system to capture youth's allegiance. Government, business, education — even the church — has not had much success in getting its message across. The church comes up for particular criticism from youth because the younger generation knows what the church teaches. Young people fail to see actions and results. As many young people see it, religion is practiced by the old as a tedious exercise without much vigor and value. The status quo seems more important than love and justice, and more effort is put into beautifying buildings than helping people. But the fault is not all the older generation's — young often fall into the status quo pattern in their youth activities.

John D. Rockefeller III said in an article in *Saturday Review*, "Young people today are committed to values of love, human dignity, individual rights, and trust in one's fellowman. These are precisely the values of our Judeo-Christian heritage. The church has been the proponent of these values for centuries. Yet no institution in our society today suffers more from the sheer indifference of the young. By and large, they have dismissed the church as archaic, ineffective, and irrelevant. One young man told me; 'There's a genuine religious revival going on, but the church is missing out on it.' Another said: 'The church could fill a great need in our society, if it would focus less on the divine and more on how to apply Christian teaching to today's world.' "[1]

The young cannot shove all the blame for the generation gap on the adult world, though adults are more experienced and should accept more responsibility. It would be sheer hypocrisy for youth to blast the older generation and say, "You made it all this way." They might have to eat many of their words after they reach the age of twenty-five. Youth need to take a good look at themselves and see if they are trying to answer many of the questions they seem so adept at asking.

Joseph T. Bayly, writing "A Word to the Now Generation," admits that his generation has problems but asks the younger set to consider their own predicament:

"We're a mess.

"But what hurts the most is this: So are you. And I suspect that's why you're so bitter about us. You hate to see the mess perpetuated in yourselves. You see your generation going down the same hypocritical path.

"You can reject our hair styles, our conformity, our ticky-tacky houses, crummy bourgeoisie tendencies, moral absolutes, etc.

"Deep down, don't you wish you could reject the hog as well, that 13-billion-dollar-a-year slice you personally spend? The soft living, plush houses, fast cars you like as much as we do?

"But that would involve sacrifice, poverty, which are things to sing about, not things to do.

"Empty words.

"Do as I sing, not as I do.

"We're fakey, but so are you. You say everything's relative, you want us to look at you in shades of gray — but then you judge us by our own absolute standard of black and white.

"Honesty is your prime virtue, if we hear you right. Then why all the cheating and shoplifting?

"You don't mean honesty like that? You mean frankness, openness about sex and morals, no pretence?

". . . Neither of us is happy, your generation or mine. No hypocrite ever is. The difference is that we're 20 years closer to the end of the game than you."[2]

Maybe the differences between the generations are exaggerated. Getting together may not be so much a question of age as a question of honesty with each other. Neither the young nor the old can claim infallibility, both are subject to the same types of human limitations. However, it is within the church of Jesus Christ that the union between young and old can become a spiritual reality. The young in the church can join with the old because they both join with Christ. All share a common Lord and a common hope.

Of course, being "one in Christ" does not guarantee perfect communion or even perfect communication. The church is composed of humans and perfect communion does not exist anywhere.

The need within the church is for all members to recognize that they belong together, that they are vital to one another, that each has something to contribute to the others because of the nature of the Holy Spirit working in individual lives.

Some young people have expressed concern that they have no voice in the issues before local congregations. Possibly this is true because of the lack of interest shown by the youth in times past — and also in the present. A solution to this problem would be for youth to attend congregational meetings. Thus they would gain the right to voice their opinions in the same manner as adults do.

Since it is youth that has emphasized the generation gap, youth also should lead the way in de-emphasizing the idea of the gap. It is not really an age gap. It is merely the normal and natural misunderstanding that comes because of poor communications between people. Where young people and adults are considerate of each other's opinions and when each looks at the other objectively, the gap ceases to exist.

When young and old believers get together, then the church will close the generation gap.

Youth in the church and in society must make
honest attempts to bridge the gap!

WHAT DOES THE BIBLE SAY?

"One generation goes and another generation comes, but the earth remains forever"
(Eccles. 1:4).

"Take pleasure, young men, in your youth
and let your heart cheer you in your youthful days; follow the ways of your heart and
the sight of your eyes, but be aware that
for all of these God will call you to account" (Eccles. 11:9).

"Be mindful of your Creator in the days of
your youth before the troubling days come
and the years draw near when you will say,
'I do not enjoy them'" (Eccles. 12:1).

"How can a young man cleanse his way? By
living in agreement with Thy word" (Ps.
119:9).

"There are those who curse their father and
do not bless their mother. There are those
who are pure in their own eyes and yet are
not washed from their filth" (Prov. 30:11,
12).

"Do not let anyone look down on you because you are young, but be an example for
the believers, in your speech, your conduct,
your love, faith, and purity" (I Tim. 4:12).

"Do not rebuke an older man, but appeal to
him as if he were your father. Treat the
younger men as your brothers, the older

women as mothers, and the younger women as sisters, with all purity" (I Tim. 5:1, 2).

"In the same way urge the young men to be self-controlled. You yourself, in all things, must be an example in good works . . ." (Titus 2:6, 7).

"In the same way, you younger men must submit yourselves to the older men. And all of you must put on the apron of humility, to serve one another; for the scripture says, 'God resists the proud, but gives grace to the humble'" (I Pet. 5:5).

"For it is through faith that all of you are God's sons in union with Christ Jesus. For you were baptized into union with Christ, and so have taken upon yourselves the qualities of Christ himself. So there is no difference between Jews and Gentiles, between slaves and free men, between men and women: you are all one in union with Christ Jesus" (Gal. 3:26-28).

WHAT DO YOU SAY?

1. How does the generation gap show itself within the church today? In what ways are you contributing to that gap? Are you right in this action? If not, how should you change?

2. How has mass media contributed to our present conflict of the generations?

3. Was Paul's admonition to Timothy about not letting his youth be despised (I Tim. 4:12), evidence of a generation gap in the early

church? What was Paul's solution? Would that solution work today?

4. In what ways do you think the church should give its youth a greater voice in the programs of the church?

5. In what specific ways do you think the church is not relating to your generation? How can this be changed?

6. Does your church place much emphasis on its youth? Whose fault is it that the youth program isn't more dynamic?

7. How does Paul's teaching concerning the unity of believers (Gal. 3:28; Eph. 2:13-16) speak against the idea of a generation gap in the church? Could the generation gap problem ever be considered a sin problem? Why or why not?

8. If gaps in life-style and values between the generations are inescapable elements of modern life, what can youth do to alleviate the strain and tension?

9. In what ways should youth respond to the ways of the older generation in order to help relieve the generation conflicts?

10. Does respect for the older generation imply obedience? If so, what is the nature of that obedience? Is it ever right to disobey adult (especially parental) leadership?

Notes

[1] John D. Rockefeller III, "In Praise of Young Revolutionaries," *Saturday Review*, December 14, 1968, p. 20.
[2] Joseph T. Bayly, "A Word to the Now Generation," *Eternity*, March 1967.

How Do You React to Society's Emphasis on Sex? 9

SEX SELLS AUTOMOBILES. Auto shows are so crowded with sexy swim-suited models, you almost fail to see the cars. Sex sells airline tickets. The "friendly skies" are filled with beautiful stewardesses. Sex sells toothpaste. Notice the way a girl catches her man after one brushing. (At least that's what the ad says.) Sex sells oriental rugs, fishing tackle, kitchen utensils, detergents and almost any product you'd like to name — except Bibles. Madison Avenue (the street in New York where most of the major advertising agencies are located) uses sex to promote everything from heavy industrial machinery to slim line reducing pills. If a manufacturer adds a little sex to an ad, especially in the form of a beautiful female, he's assured he'll sell more of the product. The American public has been brainwashed to accept sexy ads as a part of the selling game.

Most sexy display ads in our society take advantage of youth. Notice the TV ads. Unless the person is an obviously out-of-shape scrub woman who is intentionally used to show the superiority of some toilet bowl cleanser, the model usually is a beautiful, curvaceous blonde about twenty-two years old. This is a definite commercialization of sex and especially of youthful sex. Doesn't it bother you, especially you girls, that business is exploiting something that is one of your most wonderful possessions?

Maybe you aren't annoyed because our society is quite open about sex. There's a greater indulgence toward sex-oriented living. No longer is sex something that is whispered in tightly-locked bedrooms. It has become a common topic for living room conversations. Not even Christian people seem shocked by the many vulgar references to sex on TV.

Some churches are attempting to lead communities toward sex education programs that bring balance into prevalent amoral sex instruction. By providing guidance for sex education in schools, some churches have helped bring sex out of the Victorian stage and have helped many adopt a more balanced view of sex. Christian youth, then, face the choice of either submitting to grossly distorted views of sex or providing leadership in giving sex its most beautiful meanings.

To have a wholesome view of sex, you must study what the Bible says on the subject. You'll discover that God's attitude toward sex was not one of avoidance. He made sex good. It was man that corrupted it through lust. This led to the laws of the Old Testament that clearly governed relationships between the sexes. Of course, you'll find many laws that prescribe punishments for the abuse of sex, but you'll also find many passages in the Bible that present both the sanctity and beauty of sexual relationships. The Song of Solomon presents a beautiful interpretation of the meaning of sex in human relationships.

As you read biblical passages relating to this important subject, you'll discover that the Bible clearly teaches definite moral approaches to sex. This perspective is far better than the view of momentary pleasure that is prevalent in our culture.

It would be good to ask yourself: How would you react if your church began to use sexy photos to advertise your youth group programs? a choir concert? a missionary rally? Would you go along with the idea or would you oppose it? It can happen. It happened recently in England. One vicar put a photograph of a scantily clad model on the front page of his parish paper. He argued that the church can't reject glamor, therefore it ought to take advantage of the present emphasis on it. According to his thinking, his photo was in good taste. He even argued that he was actually counteracting the usually degrading displays of pornographic materials. But most of his parishioners thought differently. He didn't use any more sexy photos on the parish paper.

Some have said that the United States is suffering from a *sex*plosion. This sex binge has two main aspects. One is that sex is on the loose — moral standards are disregarded, free love is advocated, sex before marriage is condoned, and wife exchanging is accepted fun. Another aspect concerns those who uphold morality, but who have surrendered to the first group without a fight. Between these two groups stand Christians who have the task of upholding biblical chastity.

You can easily fall victim to either group. Since sex hits you from all directions, you can readily conclude that the "anything goes" attitude is acceptable. But this is a great fraud pushed on you by many self-appointed sex authorities, whose "polls" may indicate widespread practices among certain groups — especially among people who seem glad to give out the facts about sex which the majority in our society still hold as private. Such slanted facts cannot be taken as norms for behavior. On the other hand, there are the hand-wringers who say nothing can be or should be done about understanding sex behavior. Christian young people should avoid both the first extreme that says sex is everything and the second that says sex is nothing.

You should rightfully seek a better understanding of sex. Sex should be viewed from both the biblical and the scientific aspects. Sex advice that comes sprinkled with four-letter words does not represent the true and noble aspects of sex. Vulgar expressions reveal an eroticism which J. B. Priestly says is "the twanging of a single nerve to the exclusion of everything else." Sexuality that needs vulgarisms and perversions reduces God's gift of sex to mere lust. This kind of sex destroys its most beautiful and gratifying aspect — the union of two persons expressing unselfish love.

Possibly you should ask yourself the simple question: What is sex? What does it really mean to the individual? What should it mean to me today and in the future? Sex is the union of two people, not just the union of two bodies. Physical sex is a distortion of true sex if it is taken alone. As God intended sex, it is the interpenetration of two personalities, not simply the joining of two bodies. Sex without love isn't sex, it is animalism.

A Christian, contrary to much contemporary opinion, should be a vital source of truth about sex because he has learned one of the important aspects of the true union of two people. The Bible calls that union fellowship. This fellowship influences one's relationship to the opposite sex. A Christian respects the personality and character of another, therefore he maintains a high respect for the other person's body. He also keeps sex within the marriage union.

The Christian sees sex as a part of God's plan for the world. Sex is not simply the possession of a human body by another or a pair of human beings by each other. Sex has sacramental value — it accomplishes God's purposes. It is far more than a mode of pleasure. It is a gift of God to be enjoyed and shared at the proper time. It is also a gift of God for the purpose of bringing about new life.

God has His own good reasons for creating us male and female. Part of our task as humans is to appropriate our identity as sexual beings not only physically but psychologically and spiritually. By doing this, we discover the "otherness" of sex. We learn the importance of the other person. We do not look on sex from only its physical side, because sex includes the mystery of fulfillment with another person. Only in the freedom of marriage can this relationship be enjoyed to the fullest.

How you react to the sex-oriented society has great significance. It tells others what you think about your own sexuality and the sexuality of others. The commitments young people of the now generation make will have considerable influence upon their personal development and their effectiveness as leaders of tomorrow. Because sex is being exploited far out of proportion, being used as a commercial gimmick for financial gain, and being paraded as the ultimate in life without requiring commitment of one self to another, you have a responsibility to develop a wholesome view. Christian young people must take advantage of the present openness toward sex by gathering all the information they can. Along with this, they must develop a morality that will preserve true sexuality and offset the bad effects of the sex binge.

Maybe the sex binge is something you ought to protest about. Isn't it about time adults, who control advertising, book printing, moviemaking, are challenged to get off the sex binge? Why not boycott this overemphasis on cheap sex? Why not have your church youth group do something today to help bring about a more sensible, moral attitude toward sex in our culture? Since it is youth that is being exploited in the sexplosion, they have a right to protest.

WHAT DOES THE BIBLE SAY?

"So God created man in His image; in the image of God He created him; male and female He created them" (Gen. 1:27).

"Adam said, 'This at last is bone of my

bones and flesh of my flesh; she shall be called Woman because she was taken out of a man.' For this reason a man shall leave his father and his mother and cling to his wife and they shall become one flesh" (Gen. 2:23, 24).

"How beautiful are your feet in sandals, O maiden of queenly form! Your rounded thighs are a jeweled chain, the work of a master craftsman. Your navel is a rounded bowl in which mingled wine is never lacking; your belly is a heap of wheat, set about with lilies. Your breasts are as two fawns, the twins of the gazelle; Your neck is as a tower of ivory . . . How beautiful you are, my love, how lovely in that which delights! Your stature itself is a stately palm, your breasts are as clusters of grapes" (Song of Sol. 7:1-7).

"For to you the commandment is a lamp, the teaching a light, and the reproofs of discipline a way of life to keep you from the evil woman, from the smooth tongue of an unfamiliar woman. Do not lust for her beauty in your heart; neither let her eyelashes captivate you; for a harlot seeks only for a loaf of bread, but another man's wife stalks a priceless soul" (Prov. 6:23-26).

"But take up the weapons of the Lord Jesus Christ, and stop giving attention to your sinful nature, to satisfy its desires" (Rom. 13:14).

"Do not love the world or anything that belongs to the world. If you love the world, you do not have the love for the Father in you. Everything that belongs to the world — what the sinful self desires, what people see and want, and everything in this world that people are so proud of — none of this comes from the Father; it all comes from the world. The world and everything in it that men desire is passing away; but he who does what God wants lives for ever" (I John 2:15-17).

WHAT DO YOU SAY?

1. What are some good aspects of the freer emphasis on sex in our society? Has openness and "honesty" produced moral behavior?

2. In what ways does the emphasis on sex as entertainment distort the Christian view of sex? How does the use of sex in advertising take away from its meaning?

3. Since sexuality is one of the basic drives that God gave to man, why do some Christians seem reluctant to discuss it openly? Is discussion of sex something to fear or should we discuss it much like we do other aspects of life? When and where is it best to discuss sex?

4. What problems result from viewing sex as "dirty"? Why is this view not biblical? What is the biblical perspective?

5. What does the Christian mean when he says that sex is sacred? How does this differ from modern views? How can the Christian get wider acceptance for the biblical view?

6. In what ways can Christian youth slow down the overemphasis on sex in our society while still placing proper emphasis on it?

7. What alternatives can your youth group offer as replacement for any overemphasis on sex in your school or community? in advertising? Is there a legitimate use of sex in advertising? Give examples.

8. Perversions of sex dominate many current plays, novels, and movies. What can Christians do to change this? What help would come from stricter obscenity laws? How can Christian youth bring about campaigns for such laws?

9. What substitutes would you offer as replacements for much of America's preoccupation with sexual stimulation via ads, movies, tv, books, etc.?

How Free Can We Be? 10

SOME YOUNG PEOPLE are saying that everyone is entitled to absolute freedom. You can do what you want when you want to. No one else has the right to interfere. This philosophy has produced many confrontations with the law, has caused destruction of property, and has resulted in many arrests. Believers in absolute freedom decry the "restrictive establishment" and campaign for revolution that will give everyone full freedom.

The problem of how much freedom you can have didn't originate with this generation. It originated in the Garden of Eden when Eve expressed her freedom by eating the forbidden fruit. She looked at the Lord's command as an encroachment on her freedom, so she disobeyed the restriction and paid the consequences. Ever since that time man has been struggling for a balance between what he thinks is stifling determinism and obsessive freedom, between tyranny and anarchy, and between restrictive laws and libertinism. Youth are caught on the left end of the swinging pendulum. The now generation is clamoring for absolute freedom. But there are restrictive forces which are necessary to keep a healthy balance. The big question is how much freedom is healthy, how much freedom can one really have to do his own thing in a society crowded with others wanting to do their own thing?

Today's society has been quite permissive in allowing young people to experiment for themselves. Previously social taboos and social pressures put restrictions on certain activities. But today young people want the freedom to use drugs, read all types of literature, experiment with sex, and express their frustrations openly. Evidence of this is seen in protest movements, street riots, antiwar marches, modern fashions, nudity, the new morality, drug abuse, new concepts in music and art, and hair styles.

Perhaps in no other time in history have so many thought they could be completely free to do as they pleased. Many things that are popular today have the "free" label attached: free speech, free love, free art, free expression. Freedom has become a youthful obsession. In many cases this freedom has had little resemblance to the freedom our forefathers fought for. In fact, much of what passes for freedom today is nothing more than outright anarchy. For many in our day of freedom, freedom only means autonomy, it does not involve responsibility to any other person or to society. It means "doing our own thing" and limitless self-expression, regardless of how it affects others.

This freedom centers upon man himself. The idea that God is sovereign no longer holds sway over the minds of such thinkers. Some have ruled God out of the picture. Man is supreme, autonomous, and morally free to do as he pleases. Absolute laws have no meaning. Under this philosophy man works out his own problems apart from divine aid. Consequently he has great difficulty finding solutions to the problems his own freedom has created: alcoholism, drug addiction, suicide, venereal diseases, mental diseases, and a host of other personal and social problems from lung cancer to environmental pollution. Many of these can be traced to man's excessive use of his freedom. Autonomous man has asserted his freedom, but how can he escape the results?

We ought to distinguish between man's freedom and the claim to autonomy. Man is dependent, not autonomous. Man was created free to answer Yes or No to God, but he was not given the capacity of being nonanswerable to God. Man must say Yes or No to the Creator — then his freedom is governed by the answer he gives. To say No to God is to forfeit the basis of true freedom offered by God through Jesus Christ who makes a person truly free through the forgiveness of sins and the infilling of the Holy Spirit. By himself, man cannot be free from his own ego and sin. When man claims to be free from God, he becomes a slave to himself and falls into his greatest bondage.

To some, obedience to God is a denial of freedom. Here is a biblical paradox. There is no true freedom apart from service and submission to God — the Creator of freedom. Joshua aptly put it: Choose [express your freedom] this day whom you will serve [the other side of biblical freedom]. To become obsessed with self-willed freedom only brings a denial of that freedom and we become slaves. Freedom within the context of a God-controlled universe in obedience to God's Word is true freedom. "If the Son makes you free, then you will be really free" (John 8:36).

Tunis Romein, writing in *Christianity Today* said, "Choose to be a slave in the right way and be free, or choose to be free in the wrong way and be a slave."[1] The choice is quite clear, it is yours. Then you must accept the consequences.

According to the Bible, personal freedom is at the root of mankind's problems. Romans 3:23 says that all men are sinners, they have all "turned each one to his own way" (Isa. 53:6). Jesus said that all who sin are the slaves of sin (John 8:34), and proclaimed that all men could be free from their bondage only through Him. The New Testament presents the Christian as a free man, whose freedom is valued and precious. (See Gal. 2:4; 5:1, 13; I Cor. 8:9; I Pet. 2:16.)

Christian freedom is not the freedom to do anything one pleases without consideration of the consequences. Two biblical principles stand out. First, our freedom is restricted by our relationship to God (I Pet. 2:16; Matt. 22:37). God is the object of our love. This love for Him compels us to be His servants. Augustine, in effect, stated this principle when he said, "Love God and do as you please."

Secondly, our freedom is restricted by our relationship to others (I Cor. 8:9). As Christians we are concerned about how our actions affect other people. Even if we have deep insight into Christian truth and are not troubled over doubtful practices, we are to consider the other person's viewpoint and "through love be servant to one another" (Gal. 5:13). Luther's famous statement perhaps sums up the Christian perspective: "A Christian is a perfectly free lord of all, subject to none. A Christian is a perfectly dutiful servant of all, subject to all."

In deciding how you will use your freedom, you have to consider carefully God's place in your life. Is He at the center of your thinking and planning? Have you accepted the full implications of the freedom that He has offered to you? Are you free from your sins? Once you settle this matter, you will get some sense of how free you really can become. The basis of true freedom cannot be found until you have been fully related to the God of all freedom through Jesus Christ.

From this vantage point you can give the fullest consideration to your relationship to others. The amount of freedom you want for yourself is what you will want to guarantee to others. If you think you deserve more freedom than others, then there is still some weakness in your understanding of the forgiveness of God and the freedom from sin that He offers to all men.

Granting freedom to others demands that some limitations be placed on our own personal freedoms. Certain controls on freedom are necessary for the good of all truly free people. If we all "did our own thing" without regard to how we affected the people around us, and if they did the same to us, the chaos that would result would destroy our freedom to act and make us slaves to anarchy. How free are we to do our own thing? We are as free as the "golden rule" allows.

WHAT DOES THE BIBLE SAY?

"The Lord God charged the man: You may eat freely from every tree in the garden; but do not eat from the tree of knowing good and evil; for the day you eat from it you will certainly die" (Gen. 2:16, 17).

"I shall walk with freedom, for I have sought Thy precepts" (Ps. 119:45).

"All we like sheep have gone astray; we have turned each one to his own way" (Isa. 53:6).

"So Jesus said to the Jews who believed in him, 'If you obey my teaching you are really my disciples; you will know the truth, and the truth will make you free.' . . . Jesus said to them; 'I tell you the truth: everyone who sins is a slave of sin. A slave does not belong to the family always; but a son belongs there for ever. If the Son makes you free, then you will be really free'" (John 8:31-36).

"For surely you know this: when you surrender yourselves as slaves to obey someone, you are in fact the slaves of the master you obey — either of sin, which results in death, or of obedience, which results in being put right with God. . . . You were set free from sin and became the slaves of righteousness. . . . But now you have been set free from sin and are the slaves of God; as a result your life is fully dedicated to him, and at the last you will have eternal life" (Rom. 6:16-22).

"For the law of the Spirit, which brings us life in union with Christ Jesus, has set me free from the law of sin and death" (Rom. 8:2).

"Be careful, however, and do not let your freedom of action make those who are weak in the faith fall into sin" (I Cor. 8:9).

"I am a free man, nobody's slave; but I make myself everybody's slave in order to win as many as possible" (I Cor. 9:19).

" 'We are allowed to do anything,' so they say. Yes, but not everything is good. 'We are allowed to do anything' — but not everything is helpful. No one should be looking out for his own interests; but for the interests of others" (I Cor. 10:23).

". . . and where the Spirit of the Lord is present, there is freedom" (II Cor. 3:17).

"Freedom is what we have — Christ has set us free! Stand, then, as free men, and do not allow yourselves to become slaves again. . . . As for you, my brothers, you were called to be free. But do not let this freedom become an excuse for letting your physical desires rule you. Instead, let love make you serve one another. For the whole Law is summed up in one commandment: 'Love your neighbor as yourself' " (Gal. 5:1-14).

WHAT DO YOU SAY?

1. Why do young people seem to have such an obsession about "doing their own thing"?

How far should this be allowed to go? Do we need any safeguards so that doing one's own thing doesn't interfere with another's doing his own thing?

2. What is the difference between liberty and license? Does freedom need any controls? Why?

3. Is there such a thing as being absolutely free? Can we be strictly autonomous? If not, why? If so, what would be the results?

4. Should a Christian young person join "freedom" movements that are popular on college campuses?

5. How can the abuse of freedom lead to restrictions? Give some examples. How can we avoid abusing our freedoms?

6. When the Bible talks about freedom, what does it mean? What did Jesus mean in John 8: 36 when He said the Christian shall be free indeed? How does this truth make one free? Do you know it in your personal experience?

7. In what ways does the New Testament put limits on the Christian's freedom? Are these valid today?

8. What endangered the freedom of Christians in New Testament times? How did the Christians react?

9. How do legalistic tendencies among some Christians restrict true Christian freedom? What are some of these legalistic attitudes? How can they be changed?

10. In what sense is a Christian freer than the non-Christian who claims allegiance to no one?

How is the unbeliever in bondage, and how does it affect him?

11. When is a young person free to leave his parents? How much freedom should a young person have with such things as: use of the family automobile, watching TV, dating?

12. How can a person balance personal freedom as guaranteed by Christ with our commitment to obedience as His servants?

Notes

[1] Tunis Romein, "Freedom: Possession or Obsession," *Christianity Today*, January 17, 1969. Copyright 1969 by *Christianity Today*. Reprinted by permission.

Out of Shape Already? 11

THE NEXT TIME you see an adult who is out of shape, physically unfit and forced to squeeze into specially made clothing, take a good look at yourself. That unfit, obese, and out-of-shape American was once young like you and probably laid the groundwork for a size 44 at age sixteen. Physical unfitness is not only a problem of the over-thirty world. It's a disease (if it can be called that) that affects youth as well as adults.

It's a widespread myth that American youth are among the most physically fit in the world. Recent studies have shown that thousands of young people are not in good physical condition. Most young people do not get enough exercise. Dr. Kenneth Cooper, the popularizer of physical fitness through "aerobics" (exercise that demands oxygen and use of lung power) found through his studies that almost two-thirds of the Air Force recruits failed to make it into the "good" category. They were good enough to pass their initial physical, but they did not pass the standards for being in "good condition."

Like adults, thousands of young people are satisfied to let their physical condition deteriorate into a passive feeling of well-being, content to take things as they come, even though they are setting the stage in later years for heart and

107

lung diseases, high blood pressure and life-shortening obesity. There is no generation gap about fitness; it's a problem that young and old face together. But it's the young who have the advantage and are better off if they take care of themselves while they are vigorous.

Seldom in history have so many people been encouraged to be physically fit. We have received more advice about physical fitness than most of the world's people. TV, radio, books and magazines encourage Americans to jog, stop smoking, stay thin and lose excess weight. New diet programs appear almost daily. Reducing machines, mechanical exercisers and ten-day wonder diets abound. Exercise and dieting is made the cure-all for man's physical and mental problems.

In spite of all the bombardment from the nation's advertisers and health advocates, millions of Americans, young and old, are overweight, physically weak, and generally out of shape. In spite of diet foods and drinks advocated by TV commercials, we still eat too much and weigh too much. Automobiles, elevators, escalators, drive-in restaurants, drive-in banks, laundromats and other labor-saving factors have given people more time and less exercise, thus contributing to an increase of heart attacks, tension and nervous conditions.

Recent studies have shown the relationship between inactivity and certain physical diseases. It is a fact that smoking is linked to the increase in lung cancer, emphysema and other respiratory problems. High blood pressure and high cholesterol counts, both detrimental to health, have been connected with inactivity and lack of proper exercise. Physical exercise and proper diet have been shown to have a significant affect on mental and emotional health.

Americans love substitutes. They enjoy having the pleasures of life without paying the consequences. They consume synthetic foods and sugarless soda to satisfy their passion to eat and to drink. Then they take diet pills to curtail appetite. All this creates tension, which makes people eat more, smoke more and try (but fail) to relax more.

Good health requires discipline, good sense, and moderation. Very few would argue against the benefits of exercise and a good physical fitness program. Yet very few take the time to become physically fit. Many are confused about what being phsycially fit really means. Some think "feeling good" is physical fitness. Others gauge their fitness by their ability to participate in active sports. Obviously, physical fitness doesn't mean the same thing to everyone. The American Medical Association defines it as the "general capacity to respond favorably to physical effort." The important fact to keep in mind is that physical fitness is desirable not as an end in itself, but for its total effect upon a person's physical, mental and spiritual well-being.

Former President John F. Kennedy said, "Physical fitness is not only one of the most important keys to a healthy body, it is the basis of dynamic and creative intellectual activity. The relationship between the soundness of the body and the activities of mind is subtle and complex. Much is not yet understood. But we do know what the Greeks knew: that intelligence and skill can only function at the peak of their capacity when the body is healthy and strong; that hardy spirits and tough minds usually inhabit sound bodies."[1]

Christian young people who are generally concerned with their spiritual condition should ask what all this means for them. Does God expect us to spend time nurturing and developing our physical bodies? Is not all this fuss about fitness really an unnecessary and time-consuming activity? After all, doesn't the Bible say, "Physical exercise has some value in it, but spiritual exercise is valuable in every way . . ." (I Tim. 4:8)?

Modern research brings into focus an important consideration. Physical fitness has a definite relationship to a person's psychological makeup — a vital element in a Christian's overall spiritual dynamic. The Bible stresses the importance of the body. Jesus warned against letting any part of the body offend or interfere with a person's obedience to God (Matt. 5:29, 30). The apostle Paul said that he disciplined his body in order to avoid disqualification in his ministry (I Cor. 9:26, 27). He taught that the Christian's body was God's sanctuary and that God would punish those who defiled His temple (I Cor. 3:16, 17). He taught that Christians should glorify God in their bodies and in their spirits (I Cor. 6:19, 20), and intimated that while spiritual growth was primary for the Christian, bodily fitness was of value (I Tim. 4:8). These references imply an interaction between body and spirit that cannot be ignored when one considers his total commitment to God.

110

Ancient Greeks considered the body innately evil, but the mind essentially good. So long as the mind was encased in the body, it was under the sway of evil. Some early Christians adopted some of these Greek ideas. These produced monastic and celebate practices among Christians. Some Christian people still hesitate to enjoy healthful and legitimate bodily pleasures. They reason that if it feels good it must be wrong.

The Bible never justifies overindulgence or bodily satisfaction contrary to holy living. The Bible condemns using the body only for self-gratification. It not only condemns such things as excessive appetite for sex and alcohol, but also excessive appetite for food — a vice called gluttony (Prov. 23:20; Phil. 3:19). The Bible condemns abuse of the body, but not healthful and legitimate disciplines of the body. Paul's references to the Greek races and comparing these events to the Christian life shows his acquaintance with, and perhaps his enjoyment of, competitive games.

There is no direct command in the Bible to exercise or jog, but the physical demands on the lives of biblical people afforded natural exercise that we moderns do not have. They walked everywhere; we drive or ride. They expended physical effort in their daily tasks; we press buttons and pull levers. They did not have all the advantages of modern medicine to keep their bodies healthy. Sickness and disease took their lives, not because they abused their bodies, but because they were vulnerable. With modern medicines we do not die from the same diseases,

111

yet deaths and disabilities due to lack of exercise and general bodily fitness reach epidemic proportions. Diseases of the heart are the leading cause of death in the United States. They account for 39 percent of all deaths. Cardiovascular diseases all together account for about 55 percent of all deaths. Almost one million deaths a year stem from heart and respiratory problems.

Young people who are concerned about the ethical issues of war, race and poverty ought not to neglect the question of bodily health. It's ridiculous to talk about pollution of the air and water while inhaling nicotine, sipping alcohol, using abusive drugs and eating oneself to death. Those who are concerned about pollution of the air, sea and sky ought to be concerned about polluting their lungs and their blood.

Christians do not worship the body, but God says that He indwells believers and they are His temple (I Cor. 6:19). Christians who overeat, undersleep, underexercise, and who pollute their bodies with nicotine, drugs and alcohol are defiling the temple of God. Christian young people, whose bodies are at their peak of efficiency, can prolong their lives and increase their usefulness to God and to society by a balanced, healthy respect for their bodies.

WHAT DOES THE BIBLE SAY?

"Physical exercise has some value in it, but spiritual exercise is valuable in every way, for it promises life both for now and for the future" (I Tim. 4:8).

"I harden my body with blows and bring it

112

under complete control, to keep from being rejected myself after having called others to the contest" (I Cor. 9:27).

"Surely you know that you are God's temple, and that God's Spirit lives in you! So if anyone destroys God's temple, God will destroy him. For God's temple is holy, and you yourselves are his temple" (I Cor. 3: 16, 17).

"Don't you know that your body is the temple of the Holy Spirit, who lives in you, the Spirit given you by God? You do not belong to yourselves but to God; he bought you for a price. So use your bodies for God's glory" (I Cor. 6:19, 20).

"We, however, are citizens of heaven, and we eagerly wait for our Savior to come from heaven, the Lord Jesus Christ. He will change our weak mortal bodies and make them like his own glorious body, using that power by which he is able to bring all things under his rule" (Phil. 3:20, 21).

WHAT DO YOU SAY?

1. How do you define physical fitness? Why are so many young people careless about their health and bodily fitness?

2. What is the Christian view of the body? Upon this definition, where does physical fitness fit in?

3. What are the implications of the apostle Paul's attitude concerning sports and bodily fit-

ness? How does his concept of the body as the temple of God relate to physical fitness?

4. Can indifference toward physical fitness and bodily exercise be considered sinful? Why or why not?

5. How did the physical activities of Jesus and His disciples differ from our normal activities? Why do we need to supplement ordinary living with physical activities?

6. Can a person be a better Christian if he exercises and is physically fit? In what respects? Can passion for fitness be a hindrance to a Christian? How?

7. Why would some Christians have a better attitude toward life if they followed some form of exercise?

8. Are any forms of exercise — such as yoga, karate, judo or dancing questionable practices for the Christian? Why? What guidelines should Christians follow in choosing forms of exercise?

9. Does the well-being of the body have any effect on the well-being of the soul? Does the well-being of the soul have any effect on the condition of the body?

10. How does fitness relate to a Christian's testimony to the world?

11. What are the effects of tobacco, drugs and alcohol on fitness? Are these sufficient reasons not to use them?

Notes

[1]J. F. Kennedy, "The Soft American," *Sports Illustrated*, December 26, 1960. Reprinted with permission.

My Country, Right or Wrong? **12**

IT'S MIGHTY POPULAR TODAY for young people to point out the faults of America. Whether it's seemingly senseless military involvement in other countries, neglect of the poor, pollution of the air and water, big impersonal government, taxes or the military draft, someone is ready to climb on a soap box and tear down the country they live in. Others see no fault with what goes on. They have the feeling that if it's done in America it must be good. Some people say, "My country, right or wrong." They are ready to support anything the country does as long as it brings more power and prestige to the United States. However, they often fail to see long-range effects.

There is no doubt that the idea of supporting one's country, "right or wrong," is intensely loyal or patriotic. But how would we view such a statement from the mouth of a Nazi or a Russian communist? Intense loyalty and patriotism was a vital part of Germany's rise to conquer the world during the time of the Third Reich under Hitler. When we look back at the atrocities of the Nazis, it would be difficult to justify the "right or wrong" sentiment from the lips of a Christian.

Some Christians have made patriotism synonymous with religious zeal. They look upon patriotism as a Christian virtue without regard to what the ultimate implications or consequences might be. To them "God and country" are inseparable. As they look at it, God helped set up this country. God has blessed this land, and He is on our side. To oppose our nation's policies is to fight against God. To be loyal to God, we must be loyal to America, right or wrong. If God is on our side it follows that we can make no mistakes. It also follows that we should not change anything, because God helped us set it up that way in the beginning.

Not every Christian buys that concept of patriotism. It's easy to show that tyrants like Adolph Hitler thought they were on God's side too. To say, "Our country, right or wrong," as a blanket endorsement of every action of our nation, could lead to dangerous fascism. Carl Schurz, a nineteenth century American reformer, put the statement in proper perspective. He said, "Our country, right or wrong! When right, to keep right: when wrong to be put right!"

Most Christians believe that a patriotic spirit is a duty of good citizens. But, how far do you carry this spirit? Should a Christian allow his patriotism to blind him to the faults of his country? Does patriotism substitute for effective witness concerning Christ to the world? Is it possible that patriotism itself can be idolatry? There are some Christians who have made it their life mission to preserve America from the devil of communism. To them to be anticommunist is preaching the gospel.

Other Christians feel that the great task of

the believer is to be a witness to Christ's resurrection power. The Christian should not become entangled excessively with patriotism and lose his sense of mission for Christ and the church. Many would question whether God calls anyone to be anticommunist. God calls men and women to be His servants to proclaim the positive gospel of God's good news of redemption through Christ.

The Christian asks at what point does loyalty to country end and loyalty to God begin? When his country espouses a policy or action contrary to God's law, the Christian must be willing to scrutinize his country's action in the light of God's revelation in the Bible. At this point many Christians fail to bring biblical principles to bear on their nationalistic views. They reverse their loyalties and put country ahead of God. They forget that loyalty to country is conditioned by loyalty to God, not the other way around.

When Christians consider patriotism they need to find a sane and balanced view. It's no sin for Christians to be active in politics or to pledge allegiance to the flag. Many Christians sin by their inaction and uninvolvement rather than by overaction. The apostle Paul took advantage of his Roman citizenship, but did not become a slave to the Roman government. Peter urged Christians to "submit for the Lord's sake, to every human authority" (I Pet. 2:13, 14), but he obeyed God rather than submitting to man's arbitrary and unfair laws (Acts 4:19, 20; Acts 5:29). Paul (Rom. 13) made it clear that Christians are expected to be responsible citizens toward the state and even to pray for its leaders

(I Tim. 2). What does all this mean? Does it mean that we should be uncritical and compliant when our government acts irresponsibly?

Paul implies in Romans 13 that our responsibility is to responsible government. Rulers are looked upon as "terrors" toward evil, who "praise" good deeds, and who stand in judgment of evil doers. It is assumed that the government in question is based on laws and principles of justice. A government that offends God's laws and flaunts peace and justice toward all men does not deserve the support of Christians.

There are Christians today who feel that the United States does not always follow just policies. They feel America's involvement in the war in Southeast Asia is immoral. From the beginning, funds that could have been used for social improvements at home to alleviate misery and poverty have been drained for a war that means little or nothing to millions of Americans. They oppose such military actions. The governmental credibility gap has influenced many Christians to speak out against the United States' foreign policies. These people love their country deeply and are seriously concerned about some of its actions. To make their concerns known they have often taken unpopular stands that have made other Christians suspicious of them. Yet they have had the courage to speak according to their consciences.

Other Christians, in the name of patriotism, have felt that extremism used to defend our liberties is justified. They defend the controversial statement Barry Goldwater made during the 1964 presidential campaign: "Extremism in the defense of liberty is no vice." But many on the left have attempted extremism to "defend" their concepts. Both left and right are capable of extremism and violence. In a democracy there must be balance and compromise. Christians line up on both sides. It is difficult to determine what is the "Christian" view of any particular issue, but the principles of Romans 13 must be formative in the Christian's understanding. The Christian's highest loyalty is to Christ and His kingdom, but he can be active in his government and contribute to peace and justice. At times this may mean avid support for the actions his government takes, but at other times it may mean disapproval.

What divides us as a nation today is not the division of young and old, but our inability to determine whether the actions of our government are moral and just. The Christian must ask whether our nation's actions are in keeping with Scripture, for his attitude and response is determined by his obedience to God's Word. But both Christian and non-Christian alike ask whether America is right in spending billions to travel into space when twenty-two million people live at the poverty level. Is America right in fighting wars that waste billions of dollars, cost precious lives and stifle social progress at home? Is America right in developing missiles that accelerate the arms race among nations, that bring the world closer to annihilation? Where should we let our patriotism lead us? Do we become arrogantly indifferent about these issues? Or do we seek to destroy our system of government simply because we don't agree with it?

Besides, who really is responsible for the governmental leaders who are in office?

It is not enough to say "my country, right or wrong." The issues are too complex for such a simplistic approach. A democracy calls for compromise, give and take, liberty, justice, the right to be heard and the right to dissent. The Christian must act according to his conscience and according to scriptural principles. But as a Christian he still must compromise, give, take, be free, be just, speak out. But in doing all these his first allegience must be to God.

WHAT DOES THE BIBLE SAY?

"Submit yourselves, for the Lord's sake, to every human authority: to the Emperor, who is the supreme authority, and to the governors, who have been sent by him to punish evildoers and praise those who do good. For this is God's will: he wants you to silence the ignorant talk of foolish men by the good things you do. Live as free men; do not use your freedom, however, to cover up any evil, but live as God's slaves. Respect all men, love your fellow believers, fear God, and respect the Emperor" (I Pet. 2:13-17).

"Everyone must obey the state authorities; for no authority exists without God's permission, and the existing authorities have been put there by God. Whoever opposes the existing authority opposes what God has ordered; and anyone who does so will bring judgment on himself. For rulers are not to be feared by those who do· good but by those who do evil. Would you like to be unafraid of the man in authority? Then do what is good, and he will praise you. For he is God's servant working for your own good. But if you do evil, be afraid of him, for his power to punish is real. He is God's servant and carries out God's wrath on those who do evil. For this reason you must obey the authorities — not just because of God's wrath, but also as a matter of conscience. This is also the reason you pay taxes; for the authorities are working for God when they fulfil their duties. Pay, then, what you owe them; pay them your personal and property taxes, and show respect and honor for them all" (Rom. 13:1-7).

"Remind your people to submit to rulers and authorities, to obey them, to be ready to do every good thing" (Titus 3:1).

" 'Show me the coin to pay the tax!' They brought him the coin, and he asked them, 'Whose face and name are these?' 'The Emperor's,' they answered. So Jesus said to them, 'Well, then, pay to the Emperor what belongs to him, and pay to God what belongs to God' " (Matt. 22:19-21).

"Jesus answered, 'You have authority over me only because it was given to you by God . . .' " (John 19:11).

WHAT DO YOU SAY?

1. When, if ever, is the statement, "My country, right or wrong," a valid one? Can a Christian make that statement?

2. To what extent should Christian young people practice patriotism? Give some ways in which patriotism should be expressed. Can anyone become too patriotic? How?

3. Why is patriotism often associated with support of a country's involvement in war efforts? Is this right or wrong? Why? Why were the American revolutionaries in the eighteenth century patriotic?

4. How can young people express dissent and still maintain a patriotic spirit? Should Christians speak out for drastic changes in our society? If so, how?

5. Is there a specifically "Christian" form of government? Is it right to assume that the democratic form of government is more Christian than other forms? Why or why not? If not, what form of government do you think comes closest to the Christian ideal?

6. Assume that a government does not fulfil the stipulations of Romans 13. Do Christians then have the right to oppose its actions? Or should Christians submit to the dictates of whatever government they are under, national, state or local?

7. How does the Christian's dual citizenship (Phil. 3:20) relate to our actions as Christians in society and political life? Should a Christian ever renounce national loyalties?

8. Paul accepted the benefits of Roman citizenship and appealed to it to obtain his civil rights (Acts 22:25-29). What applications does this have to our relationship to our government? What personal responsibilities are involved on our part?

9. Should Christians join anticommunist efforts? Why or why not? Would we be free today if others hadn't taken a stand against totalitarianism?

10. What are some of the ways you as a Christian express your support for your country?

Date Due

Code 4386-04, CLS-4, Broadman Supplies, Nashville, Tenn., Printed in U.S.A.